Renew by phone or online
777

Oh My Goddess!

ああっ女神さまっ

4

STORY AND ART BY
Kosuke Fujishima

TRANSLATION BY
Dana Lewis, Alan Gleason,
AND Toren Smith

LETTERING AND TOUCH-UP BY
Susie Lee AND Betty Dong
WITH Tom

D0260456

1801020611

TIT

WHO'S WHO
IN OH MY GODDESS!

KEIICHI MORISATO — Student. Doofus. "The Mack Man". He was quite content to enjoy the quiet life before the sudden arrival of a magical being named Belldandy... now all he wants is some time alone with her... and away from Urd!

BELLDANDY — Goddess. Beauty. Granter of wishes. When Keiichi accidentally dials the Goddess Technical Hotline, he inadvertently summons Belldandy into his dorm room. Her only goal in life is to make everybody happy now she's a part of humanity.

SAYOKO MISHIMA — Queen of the campus. Has all the stunning looks, intelligence and sophistication you'd expect of someone constantly hounded by potential suitors. The arrival of a certain goddess has disturbed her supremacy — now she must derail Keiichi's relationship with her to regain it!

URD — Bell's mischievous sister. Her frequent efforts to bring Keichii and Bell together often cause more trouble than it's worth!

TOSHIYUKI AOSHIMA — The new guy on campus... one with a roving eye for a certain mystical lady!

MEGUMI MORISATO — Keiichi's sister. Currently parked outside of Keichii's place.

MARA — Trouble comes in small packages... particularly those that are round, shiny, and looking not unlike a compact disc...

CHAPTER 24

The Flying Motor Club

IN THE LAST DAYS OF WORLD WAR II, THE JAPANESE NAVY WORKED TO DEVELOP AN EXPERIMENTAL FIGHTER PLANE TO INTERCEPT AMERICAN B-29 BOMBERS. IT WAS CALLED THE *SHINDEN.*
BUT ITS FIRST TEST FLIGHT CAME LESS THAN TWO WEEKS BEFORE JAPAN'S SURRENDER-- AND HENCE IT NEVER HAD THE CHANCE TO PROVE ITSELF IN BATTLE.
THE *SHINDEN*, OR "MAGNIFICENT LIGHTNING," FEATURED AN UNUSUAL REAR-WING, PUSHER-PROP CONFIGURATION.
...IT REMINDS ME OF FLYING MY GRANDPA'S PLANE...
TODAY THE ONLY KNOWN REMAINING *SHINDEN* IS HOUSED AT THE NATIONAL AIR & SPACE MUSEUM IN WASHINGTON, D.C.
十八試局地戦闘

IT DIDN'T LOOK ANYTHING LIKE THE *SHINDEN* ...BUT THE BLUE SKY WAS THE SAME...
YEAH... HE EVEN LET ME TAKE THE CONTROLS A FEW TIMES...

WAKE UP, FOOL!

ONLY *TEN DAYS* T' DA NEXT *CAMPUS FESTIVAL!!* WE NEED TA *ADVERTISE!*
THIS THING DON'T GOT NO ENGINE!
SO? FIND A LAWN-MOWER!
DIRT CHEAP
UNDERSOLD!!

SO PUT ON DIS *MOLDY, STINKIN'* OLD *COS-TUME...*
...TRY NOT TA *PUKE,* AN' GET OUT DERE AN' *SPREAD DA WORD!*

!!
DON'T MAKE ME GO IN THERE! HEAVE! RETCH!
UM...

WE THOUGHT WE'D TRY TO COLOR-COORDINATE OUR OUTFITS--WHAT DO YOU THINK?
I THINK IT LOOKS GREAT. WHAT DO *YOU* THINK?
choke!
wheeze!
STOMPA
ALERT!!
ALERT!!
STOMPA
STOMPA
STOMPA

AOSHIMA... HAS BETRAYED US!
STABBED US IN THE BACK!!

N.I.T. F.W.C.
NEKOMI INSTITUTE OF TECHNOLO
FOUR WHEELS CLUB
入会受け付け中
NIT FWC
SIGN UP HERE!
NOW WELCOMING NEW MEMBERS... IT'S THE NEKOMI TECH FOUR WHEELS CLUB PRE-FESTIVAL SIGN-UP!
KOENIG
PRINTED BY HOLBEIN & EXEN.

SO SIGN YOUR NAME ON THIS SIMPLE MEMBERSHIP FORM...
MEMBERSHIP APPLICATION
NAME:
CLASS:
DEPT:
AGE:
SEX: M F
I, ______, HEREBY SELL MY SOUL TO THE N.I.T. FOUR WHEELS CLUB.
SIGNED:

BUT IF YOU THINK OUR GIRLS LOOK GOOD... JUST LOOK AT OUR CARS!

UNLIKE CERTAIN PATHETIC MOTOR CLUBS WE COULD MENTION...
...OUR CLUB HAS EVEN MORE CUTE GIRLS!!

huff huff
MUST... SELL...SOUL...
TAMIYA! HEY! NO! THAT'S WRONG!

ME FIRST!
NO, ME!
GET IN LINE!!
HEH-HEH-HEH.

YOUR CLUB'S DAYS ARE NUMBERED, AND YOU *KNOW* IT!
THAT'S RIGHT, BOYS... *MARCH FORTH!*

AT EASE, TROOPS!!
YES, *SIR!!*

SO KEEP THINKIN' O' *IDEAS!* USE YUH *BRAIN!*
REMEMBER DA MOTOR CLUB *MOTTO-- "GREAT DEEDS IS DONE WIT' NO BUDGET"!*

DAT'S RIGHT! JUST LIKE *I* DO!
BRAINS! BRAINS! BRAINS!

THEN I CAN FINALLY WREST BELLDANDY FROM YOUR GRUBBY CLUTCHES...
...AND INTO *MY* GRUBBY CLUTCHES!!

YOU NOTICED?! I *TELL* YOU-- NO BUNCHA LITTLE COED CHICKIES ARE GONNA UPSTAGE *ME!!*

JUST WAIT AND *SEE!*

YEAH... WE MAY NOT HAVE MONEY, BUT WE HAVE *GODDESS-ES!*

A-ARE YOU GONNA WEAR THAT HOME?

WHY *NOT?*

I THINK IT LOOKS *GOOD* ON ME!

GOOD LOOKS, BUT NOT GOOD LUCK...

THE NEXT DAY
WHAT? I DON'T REMEMBER OUR CLUBHOUSE BEIN' LIKE DIS!!

DID WE HAVE A PARTY LAST NITE OR SUMTIN'?
thmp

DIG! DIG FOR SAL-VAGE!
DERE'S GOTTA BE SOMETHIN' LEFT WE CAN USE!
FOR WHAT? LAND-FILL...?
Make Thyself Known to Me...
...O Buried Treasure!
Heed My Voice and Answer!

Here... Here I am...
WAIT-- THERE'S SOME-THING BURIED RIGHT HERE!
SAY WHUT?!

YOU *HEARD* DA CHICK! *DIG* DIS CRAZY SCENE!
THMP THMP
BRTTTTTT
CHOKCHOK
WE'RE NOW THE "DAY LABORERS" CLUB...
猫実

IT'S A *MYSTERIOUS OBJECT! LIFT!!*
CHAK CHAK
WHAT THE... HOLY CRAP!!

I..I DON'T BELIEVE IT!! IT'S... IT'S...
...A SHINDEN!!
HA! HOW COME IT DON'T GOT NO PROP ON FRONT, THEN?
ON THE BACK, TAMIYA... THE SHINDEN HAD A PROP ON THE BACK...
BUT WAIT A SEC...THE CAMPUS WAS BUILT ON THE SITE OF AN OLD NAVAL AIR STATION...
...B-BUT THE ONLY SHINDEN'S SUPPOSED TO BE IN AMERICA!!
Speak to Me.
Why Are You Here?
Why Were You Buried?

I am *Shinden II*, the second prototype. I was made to soar through the sky...
...But I was deprived of my destiny...

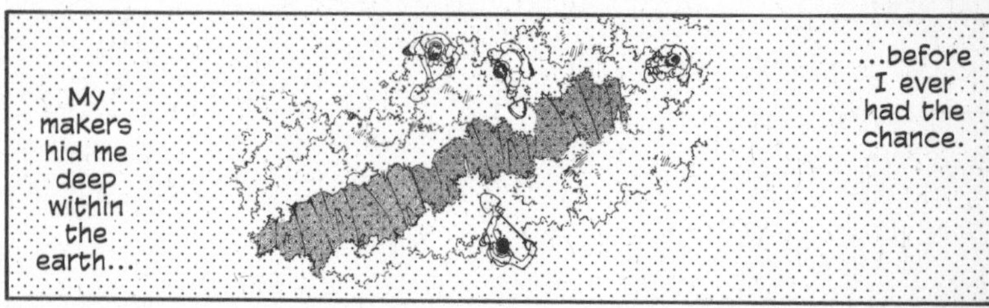
My makers hid me deep within the earth...
...before I ever had the chance.

KEIICHI...
I beg thee, let me fly.

...LET'S GIVE THE *SHINDEN* A CHANCE!
HUH ?!

DAT'S *IT!!*
Kyaa!

DIS PLANE IS DA ONLY ONE OUTSIDE A MUSEUM, RIGHT?!
SO IT'S SUMDIN' DA FOUR WHEELS CLUB CAN'T BUY!
WE GET DIS THING FLYIN', WE'LL BE DA WONDER A DA' CAMPUS!
DAT'S RIGHT! DEY'LL WONDER ABOUT US!

I DUNNO, TAMIYA... WE'RE A MOTOR VEHICLE CLUB, NOT A FLYING CLUB.
NEKOMI TECH MOTOR C

PSHAW! CONSULT DA DICTION-ARY!
mo·tor ve·hi·cle (n.) a wheeled transport commonly propelled by an internal combustion engine.

YEAH! HOW YOU LIKE THEM APPLES!
IT'S GOT WHEELS AND AN ENGINE!

EXCEPT IT'S GOT NEITHER WHEELS...
...NOR AN ENGINE.
HMMM! EXCELLENT POINT!

DIG IT, MAN!
WELL DEN, BACK TA SUMTIN' WE *KNOW* WE'RE GOOD AT-- ***DITCH DIGGIN'!***
WAIT !!
YOU WON'T GET ANYWHERE JUST DIGGING AT RANDOM...

DON'T WORRY...THE *SHINDEN* SAYS ***ALL*** OF HIS PARTS ARE HIDDEN ELSEWHERE NEARBY.

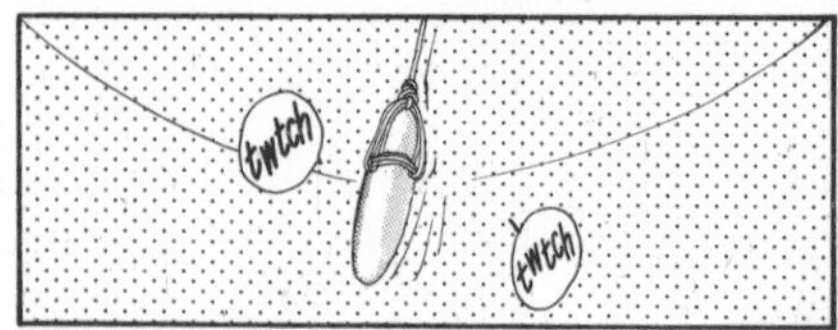
twtch
twtch

Wings, O Wings...
WHOA! ***DOWSIN'***, EH?
twtch twtch
twtch
HERE!

MEN! WE SEEK OUT BURIED TREASURE!
GOOD LUCK!

KNOCK BEFORE ENTERING
OCTOBER 3-18
RAIN OR SHINE
COME CHEER US TO VICTORY!
WOMEN'S VOLLEYBALL CLUB
WANTED!!
A CUTE GUY TO BE OUR MANAGER
WE'RE WAITING!
EASY WORK!
GOOD PAY!
PRETTY GIRLS
LOTSA FUN!

WHAT'S ALL THAT GRUNT-ING OUT BACK?
?

um
STOR
KEEP
um

CHIMPS? GORIL-LAS?
NO

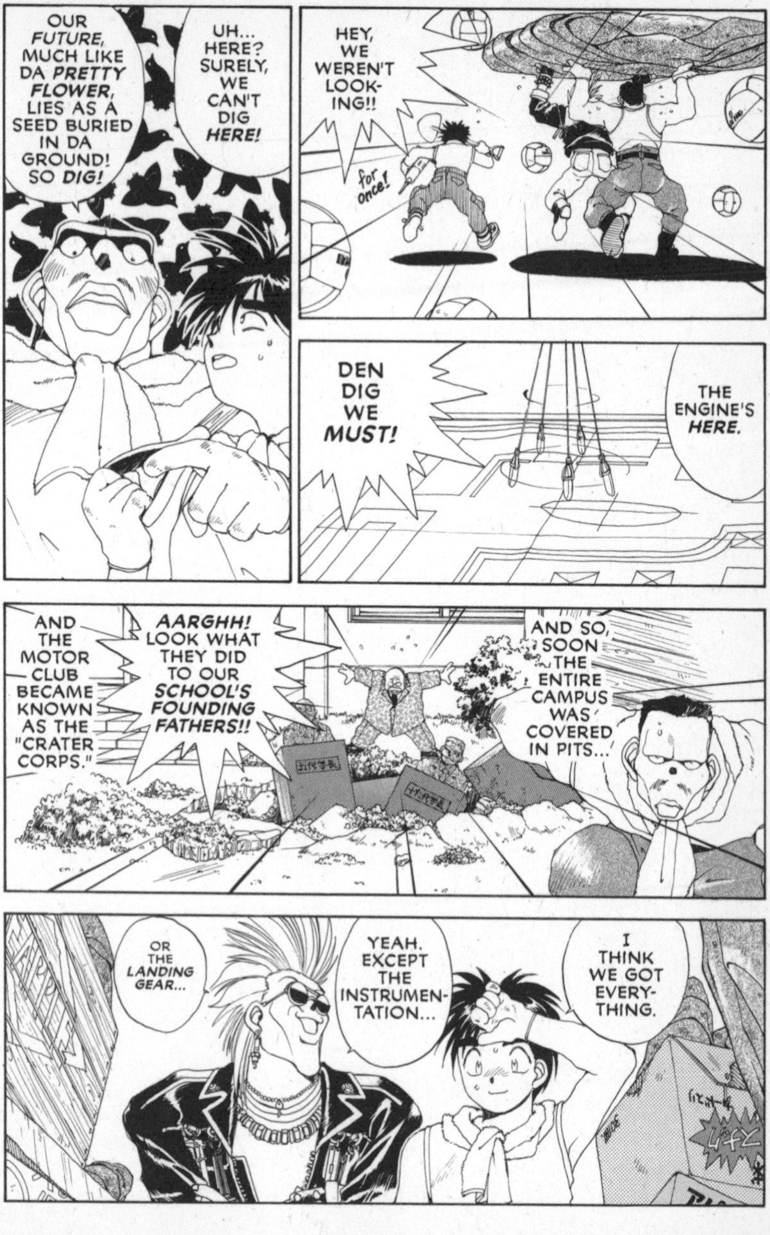

OUR *FUTURE*, MUCH LIKE DA *PRETTY FLOWER*, LIES AS A SEED BURIED IN DA GROUND! SO *DIG!*

UH... HERE? SURELY, WE CAN'T DIG *HERE!*

HEY, WE WEREN'T LOOKING!!

for once!

DEN DIG WE *MUST!*

THE ENGINE'S *HERE.*

BUT DON'T WORRY, YOU CAN LEAVE THOSE LITTLE DETAILS TO US!
HUH ?!
YEAH, YOUSE GOT FAR BIGGER WORRIES, MORISATO! LIKE YOUR TRAINING!

T-T-TRAINING...? WHAT FOR?!
HA-HA! WHAT FOR, HE SAYS! FOR DA SHINDEN, OF COURSE!
shiver
shiver

B-BUT I DON'T HAVE A PILOT'S LICENSE!
SO? WE'RE YOUR FRIENDS! WE'LL NEVER TELL!
NO! HELP!!!!

BELL-DANDYYY !!

I SENSE THAT SOMEHOW HE'LL DO FINE.
...YOU'LL BE FLYING SOON...
...SHINDEN.

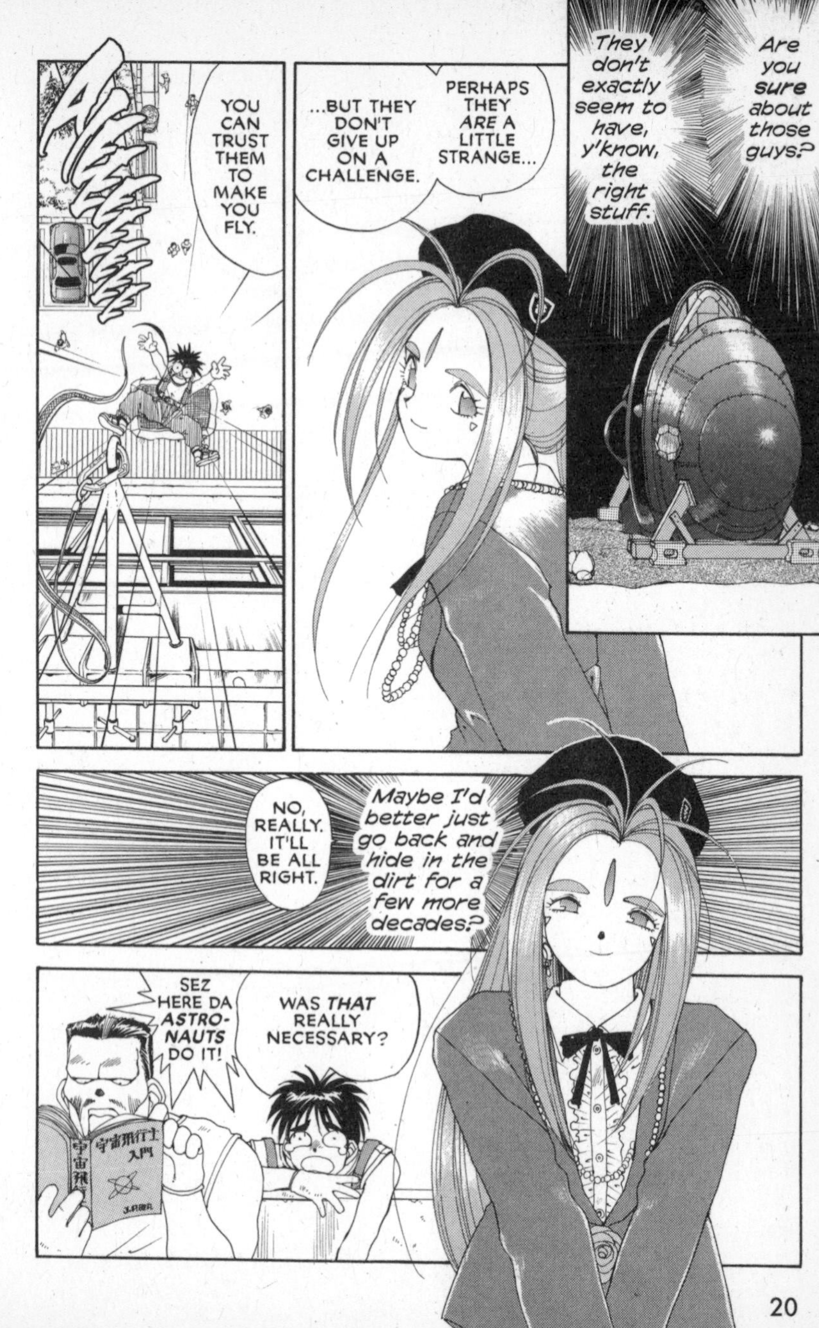
Are you sure about those guys?
They don't exactly seem to have, y'know, the right stuff.
PERHAPS THEY *ARE* A LITTLE STRANGE...
...BUT THEY DON'T GIVE UP ON A CHALLENGE.
YOU CAN TRUST THEM TO MAKE YOU FLY.
Maybe I'd better just go back and hide in the dirt for a few more decades?
NO, REALLY. IT'LL BE ALL RIGHT.
WAS *THAT* REALLY NECESSARY?
SEZ HERE DA *ASTRONAUTS* DO IT!

AIEEEEEEEE
LOOKS LIKE THEY'RE ACTUALLY PLANNING TO TRY AND FLY THAT HEAP.
LISTEN TO THEM.
EVEN FOR *LUNATICS*, THEY'RE LUNATICS.
WELL, AT LEAST A HIDEOUS CRASH WILL LIVEN UP THE FESTIVAL!
THE NEXT DAY
36TH NEKOMI FESTIVAL
NEW MEMBERS ARE **ALSO** ALLOWED ONE FREE **OGLE!**
THE AMAZING SHINDEN FIGHTER FLIES AGAIN!!
ADMISSION ¥200-

VREEEEE
chakka chakka

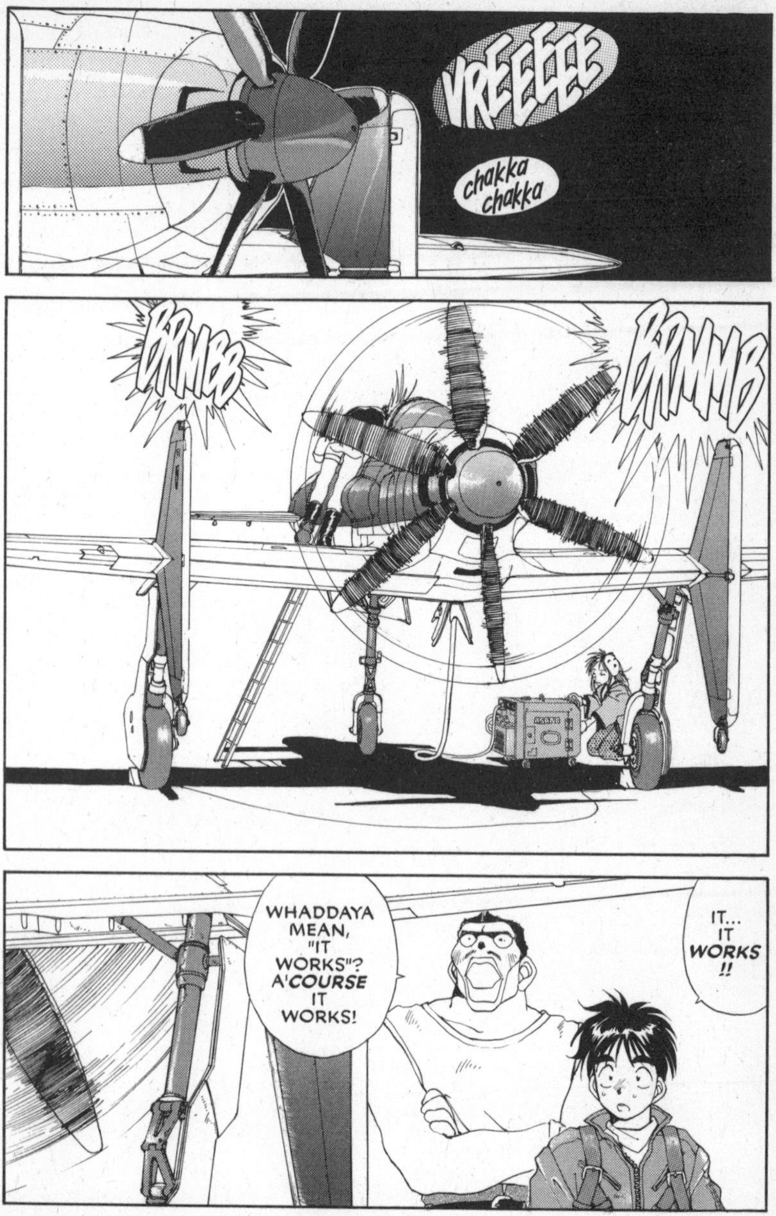

BRMMB

BRMBB

IT... IT WORKS!!
WHADDAYA MEAN, "IT WORKS"? A'COURSE IT WORKS!

I ADMIT WE *GUESSED* ONNA FEW PARTS, AN'...
WHERE *YOU* GOIN', MORISATO?
!!
HE'S A *MORON*, YES...BUT NO ONE COULD DENY HIS *COURAGE!*
krnch krnch
MAN, I'M DOOMED. JUST BECAUSE I FLEW A PLANE STRAIGHT AND LEVEL *TEN YEARS* AGO...
...DOESN'T MEAN I KNOW ANYTHING ABOUT *TAKING OFF!*

KEIICHI!

TAKE GOOD CARE OF THE *SHINDEN!*
IF YOU GIVE HIM A CHANCE TO FLY...
...I'M *SURE* HE'LL HELP YOU OUT!

LEAVE IT TO ME, BELL-DANDY!
HOW CAN I REFUSE... A MISSION FROM A *GODDESS?!*
pat
....

BRAAAAAAA

LET'S GO, SHIN-DEN!!
chak
OKAY, THEN...
GREAT... THEY JUST BOLTED ON A BUNCH OF *MOTOR-CYCLE* AND *TRUCK* GAUGES...
WELL... AT LEAST I CAN READ THEM...

WHRRRRRRRRRR
NIT MCC

HEY, UH...
...HE'S SURE EATIN' UP A LOTTA *RUNWAY,* AIN'T HE?

AARG!
WHAT'S WRONG? WHY CAN'T WE TAKE OFF?!

The pitch...
WHAT?
You wanna end up underground, too? Change the **pitch!**

ROGER! CHANGING THE PROPELLER PITCH!!
Genius! **Genius,** this kid!

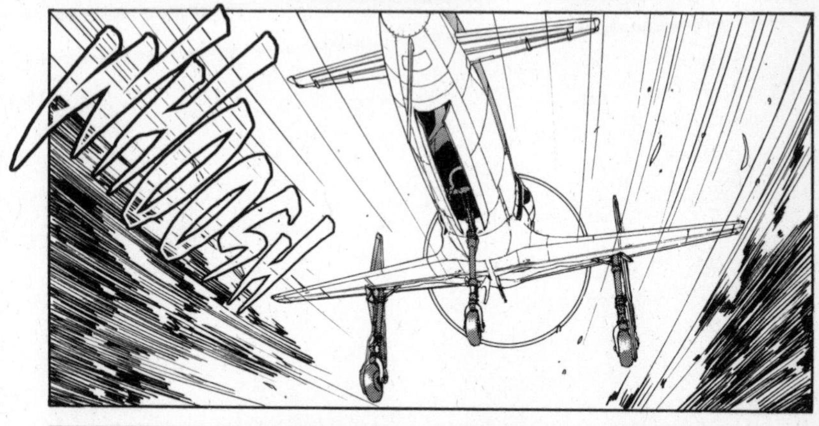

HURAAAAAAAH!

WOW...

YOU REALLY DID WANT TO FLY... DIDN'T YOU, SHINDEN?

THE SHINDEN'S GREEN FUSELAGE SHIMMERED IN JOY... AS IT SOARED INTO THE CLEAR BLUE SKY...

THE ADVENTURES OF MINI-URD

PART 2

1/24

1/35

SEE YOU NEXT TIME!

....
The Nectar of Love is Sweet...
The Flower of Love is Crimson...
FWSSH
HEH...
Boil, Boil, O Nectar of Love!
Bloom, Bloom, O Flower of Love!

Entwine in Passionate Embrace and Form the SEEDS OF LOVE!
CHAPTER 25
Let's Take the Love Seeds

チョコクリス
健康食品またんご
無農薬
GRAPE
We are

Appear Now in My Hand!!

BOMF!

HEE-HEE-HEE...
IF I CAN JUST GET KEIICHI TO TAKE THIS...

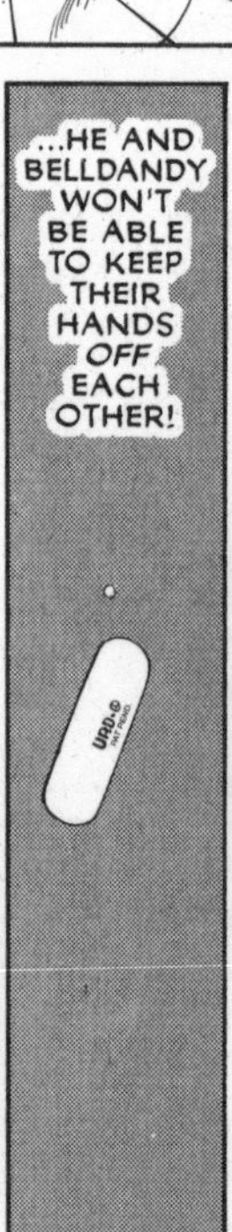
...HE AND BELLDANDY WON'T BE ABLE TO KEEP THEIR HANDS OFF EACH OTHER!

I CAN HARDLY WAIT!!!

POP

WHAT-CHA-DOON?
YO, URD!
OKAY... THE SEED IS IN THE TEA...
sshh

HEYYYY...
...WOULD YOU LIKE SOME TEA?

?
APE? MONKEY? YETI? OH, WAIT.. HE'S ONE OF KEIICHI'S BUDDIES. HMMM...

WHO ARE--

shloop
shloop
shloop
...I GUESS HE'LL COUNT AS A HUMAN TEST SUBJECT!

GLUG!
but
but
but
UM, DUHHHH... YEAH!
SURE!!
GRAB!
but...
OH, WELL... AT LEAST I'VE STILL GOT A CUP FULL.
TASTY!
HEY... IT'S NOT AFFECTING HIM AT ALL!
AIN'TCHA GONNA HAVE SOME, URD?
um...
WELL, UH, THAT IS...

HEY, LOOK!!

WHAT WAS THAT?!

BLAM!

GULP!

NO! STOP!!

WHAT WAS IN THE TEA, SIS? IT WAS LOVE SEEDS, WASN'T IT?!
muh
UH-OH! OUR FELLOW STU-DENTS!
MUTTER MUTTER

C'MON... WHILE WE STILL GOT A SCAPE-GOAT!!

A MYSTE-RIOUS EXPLO-SION!
WHAT CAUSED IT?
THERE!

TAMIYA!

THAT EXPLAINS IT!
OBVIOUSLY, HE MUST BE TO BLAME!

SO, WHAT EXACTLY ARE THESE "LOVE SEEDS"?

WELL, THE SHORT ANSWER IS...
...IT'S A KIND OF APHRO-DISIAC.
A-A-APHRO-DISIAC?

IT INFLAMES DESIRE...IN THE CASE OF HER FORMULA, ACTIVATED BY THE USE OF CERTAIN WORDS OR IMAGES...
ACTUALLY, I KNEW WHAT IT MEANT... I WAS JUST KIND OF SURPRISED THAT YOU DID...

BUT YOU GIVE IT TO ANOTHER PERSON... WHY WOULD SHE DRINK IT?
yeh

?
uh huh
WHO CARES ?!

THINK! IF SHE LATCHES HERSELF ONTO SOME GUY... MAYBE SHE'LL FINALLY LEAVE US ALONE!
HO HO HO!

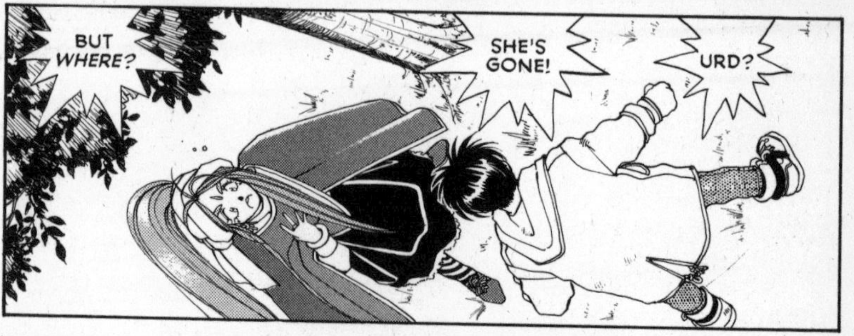

PLUM BLOSSOMS...

WHAT ?!
YO, URD, I'M LEAVIN' ON A QUEST FOR THE GOLDEN BUSH WARBLER.
THE MAN I LOVED SO LONG AGO WAS THE SPIRIT OF A PLUM TREE.
BUT... BUT... WHAT ABOUT US?!
SORRY, BABE... BUT A PLUM SPIRIT'S GOTTA DO WHAT A PLUM SPIRIT'S GOTTA DO...IN THIS CASE... QUEST FOR THE GOLDEN BUSH WARBLER.
FARE-WELL!
I REALLY LIKED HIM... EVEN IF HE WAS A LITTLE WEIRD...
THE LOVE SEEDS HAD NOW BEEN ACTIVA-TED...
AIEEE
HE ALWAYS FORGETS HE CAN'T FLY...

TH- THAT OLD COOT OVER THERE...

STOMP STOMP

uh... uh, uh... M-M-MIND IF I JOIN YOU?

?

AY!

GOT SOMETHIN' FOR YA, MORI-SATO...

LOOK, OTAKI, I'M KINDA *BUSY* RIGHT NOW--

HEY, WAIT...

...*URD* ?!

NOT TOO BUSY FOR *THIS!* OUR FIRST BATCH OF *MOTOR CLUB SWEAT-SHIRTS!*
NOTE IT BEARS THE *PLUM* KANJI... SYMBOLIC OF...OF THE *PLUM!!*
WE GOT 'EM IN S, M, AND XXXL!
ONLY 2500 YEN EACH IF YOU BUY *NOW...*
SALES TAX *NOT* INCLUDED...

MY DEAR PROFES-SOR...
...I FIND I'VE FALLEN IN LOVE...
...WITH THE WISDOM IN YOUR EYES.
I KNOW... THAT RING BINDS YOU TO ANOTHER...
...BUT JUST FOR THIS DAY... LET US PRETEND...
URD!
SNATCH
S-SORRY ABOUT THAT, SIR!

KIDS NOWDAYS... THEY'VE GOT A PRETTY STRANGE SENSE OF HUMOR.
BUT, STILL...
Chik
...THAT MADE ME FEEL YOUNG AGAIN...
...FOR ABOUT TEN SECONDS.
LET ME GO!

MY HEART IS BRREEEAAAK-INNNG!!!
I LOVE HIM! I LOVE HIM!!!
OW! HE'S GOT A WIFE! GRAND-KIDS!

BAR-RIER UP!
WOOSH
TRIFLE WITH MY AFFECTIONS, WILL YOU?!
ZANK
WHEW... JUST IN TIME!
koff koff

DAMN! WE LOST HER AGAIN!

WHEN SHE GOES OFF LIKE THAT, THERE'S NO TELLING *WHAT* WILL HAPPEN!
EH?

DON'T WORRY, KEIICHI. I PLANTED A TRANSMITTER ON HER. WE'LL FIND HER IN NO TIME!
beeeeep beeeeep

HMPH!! DON'T THEY CARE FOR A YOUNG MAIDEN'S *FEEL-INGS?!*

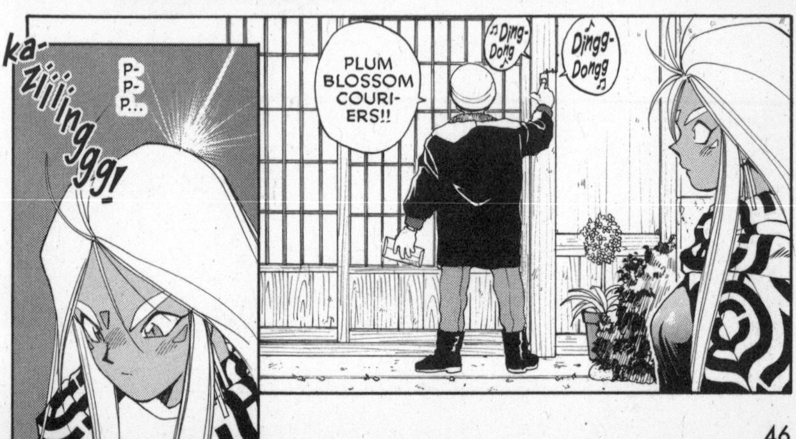
Djing-Dong
Djingg-Dongg
PLUM BLOSSOM COURI-ERS!!
P-P-P...
ka-ziiiingggg!

PLEASE, MR. POSTMAN!

yes? hello?
WELL, UH...
...EXCUSE ME, WHO ARE YOU?
CAN YOU FIND... SOMEWHERE IN YOUR PACKAGES AND PARCELS...
...A LETTER HOLDING LOVE FOR ME...?
HOW I'VE WAITED BY THE MAILBOX... FOR A HEART WITH POSTAGE DUE...

WHA--?!
...AND SO...GIVE ME YOUR *SPECIAL DELIVERY*... **NOW.**
HMMM... MAYBE *THIS* GUY WILL BE SAFE FOR HER...

I--

Now Let Me Speak Through Thee...

--That Our Two Voices May Inter-twine!

Make My Voice Thine, and Thy Voice Mine--

URD! YOU'RE A *SHAME-LESS* HUSSY!

...?!

I...I...

NOT TOO BAD, DO YOU THINK, KEIICHI?

THE AI-AI IS A TINY PRIMATE (BODY: 15 INCHES; TAIL: 23 INCHES) INDIGENOUS TO THE ISLAND OF MADAGASCAR.

IT USES ITS LONG FINGERS TO EAT FRUIT AND CATCH INSECTS.

"AI-AI" ...? I... I...
BELL-DANDY'S DOING THIS TO ME!

oops
UM...

...AW ...WHY ASK WHY...?

!
?
BUT I WON'T LET MERE WORDS COME BETWEEN US, MY DARLING!

!!
...IN AN EXISTENTIALIST SENSE, ONE PLUMBS THE DEPTHS OF DESPAIR, OR AS SARTRE PUTS IT...

...OOOH... A PHILOSOPHY MAJOR...
...SO SEXY WITH HIS CLOVE CIGARETTES !!!

SO... WHERE'S MY LETTER?
MAN... SHE SURE IS FICKLE!
L'AMOUR, C'EST ABSURD!

OUTTA MY WAY! I'VE GOT A DATE WITH THE *PROFOUND!!*

HEY YOU! WITH THE GLASSES !!
HUH?

DADDY, WE WAS S'POSED TO GO T' THE ZOO!
SORRY, HONEY... I *PLUMB* FORGOT ABOUT IT.
WHOOOSH

HOW SWEET... A MARRIED COUPLE WITH CHILD... THAT'S WHAT I WANT...
DADDY! WHEN KIN WE GO?!

I WANT A REAL FAMILY MAN!!
THAT'S WHAT I WANT! NOW!
ALTHOUGH I DON'T SUPPOSE THINGS COULD GET ANY WORSE, WE'VE GOT TO FIND HER!
plop!
I'LL GO THAT WAY!
AND JUST WHO MIGHT THIS BE, DEAR?!
I D-DON'T KNOW HER...
OH, NO-- THE TRANSMITTER FELL OFF!!
um...

URD! WHERE'D SHE GO--?
I SHOULDN'T HAVE PUT ON THIS STUPID THING...
...I'M SWEATING SO MUCH...
haa
haa
NOT AS MUCH AS I AM.
WH...
...URD...
PLUM.
PLUM !!

YOU WERE *REALLY* WORRIED ABOUT ME, WEREN'T YOU...?
I-I *WAS* ...?
ulp
OHH... I'VE ALWAYS LOVED YOU...
...KEIICHI, MY DARLING.
...ALWAYS.

UNH !?!

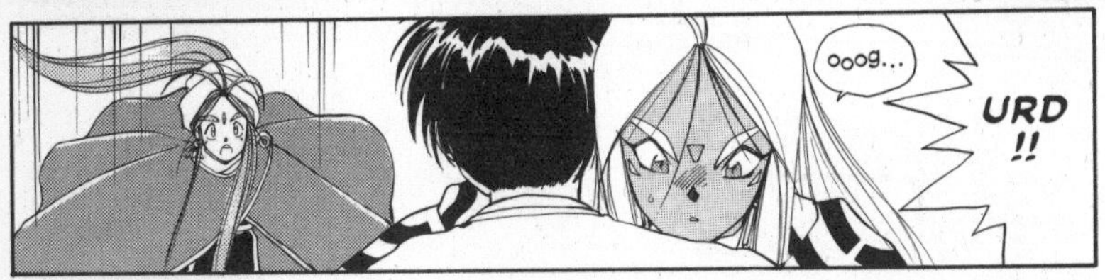
URD !!
ooog...

E-EVEN IF YOU *ARE* MY BIG SISTER...
...I-I JUST CAN'T LET YOU...
huh?
...T-TAKE MY KEIICHI.
HE'S...
HE'S MY...

DON'T BE SILLY.

I WAS JUST KID-DING.

MY...

pat

C'MON--LET'S GO HOME!

what was...

I WON-DER...

...IF SHE REALLY *WAS* JUST KIDDING...

ANTIDOTE AMULET: Cancels the effect of love seeds.

BACK! *BACK!*

BUT MEAN-WHILE, THE EFFECT HAD *FINALLY* KICKED IN FOR *TAMIYA*...

OTAKI... I KNOW *YER* A MAN...AN' *I'M* A MAN...

CHAPTER 26
The Nemesis
GODDESS
URD

...INTO ONE AS HIDEOUS AS MY OWN!!

EEE YAAAAA

haa
haa
haa

WHOA...
...THAT WAS *SOME* NIGHT-MARE.

RMMBBL

I FEEL A DISTURB-ANCE ON THE NET...

...AND IF IT *IS* WHO I *FEAR*...

...WE COULD *ALL* BE IN *GREAT DANGER!*

'SCUSE ME... D'YUH HAVE DA SINGLE "WHAT A MAN'S GOTTA DO"...?

IN THE BACK ON THE RIGHT.

UH?

A S-STRANGE F-FORCE ...! FROM DA CD...!
IT AIN'T ALL THAT POWERFUL... BUT IT'S ENUFF TA CONTROL MY BRAIN!

THAT'LL BE ¥4,800.
TAKE... CD HOME...
THANK YOU, COME AGAIN!
REIO

WEIRD... I DON'T EVEN REMEMBER GETTING THAT CD IN...

NEKOMI MEN'S DORM
NO GURLS ALOWD

HUH?
DEMONS & GODS

WHUT'S DIS?!
I DON'T REMEMBER BUYIN' IT!

I DON'T REMEMBER HAVIN' A CD PLAYER, EITHER!

BUT HEY!
I'LL PUT IT ON DA OL' TURN-TABLE! YA NEVER KNOW!

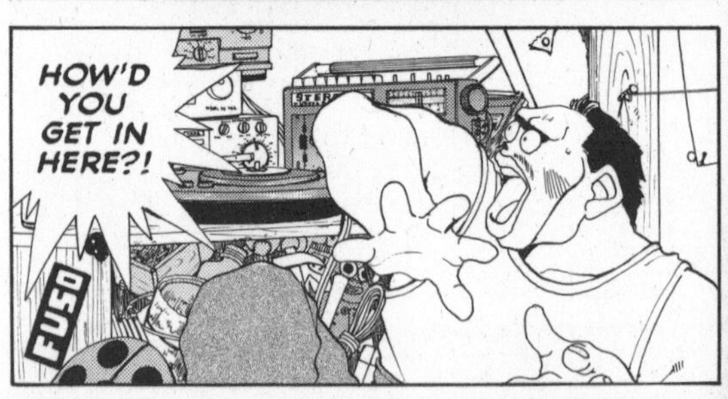
HOW'D YOU GET IN HERE?!
FUSO

I MEAN HERE...
oof
...INTO COLLEGE, I MEAN. TRYING TO PLAY A CD ON A RECORD PLAYER...WHAT ARE YOU, SOME KIND OF LOW-BROWED MORON...?
STEREO

THE NAME'S *MARA*. I'M A *DEMON* FIRST-CLASS, UNLIMITED.
AND SINCE YOU *SUMMONED* ME...
...I'LL RETURN THE FAVOR... AND GRANT YOU EXACTLY *ONE* WISH!

HOWJUH GET *IN* HERE?!

I WANTCHA T' GET OUT *RITE NOW* !!!

VERY WELL... YOUR WISH IS GRANTED.

NOT A VERY INSPIRED CHOICE, I MUST SAY.

WOOSH

!!

D-DAT WAS SO SCARY, MUH EYES EMERGED FROM DERE *PROTECTIVE BONE RIDGES!!!*

HEH HEH HEH! FAR BE IT FROM *MARA*, TOP AGENT OF THE *DEMON REALM*...

...TO LET THESE GODDESSES DO AS THEY *PLEASE!*

THAK!

THOK!

BAR-RIER UP!!

FZZAK

KEIICHI, YOU *MUSTN'T* STEP OUT OF THIS HOUSE TILL I RETURN, OKAY?

I CAN'T TRACK THE DISTURBANCE FROM INSIDE THE BARRIER, SO I'VE GOT TO GO OUT.

THOSE WAVES MUST BELONG TO MARA... I'M SURE OF IT.

MARA MAY EVEN BE HERE ALREADY...

"MARA," HUH...
...SOUNDS LIKE SHE ***KNOWS*** THIS GUY.

DAMN *RIGHT* SHE DOES!
!!
SORRY FOR THE LANGUAGE, BUT I *AM* A DEMON.

BETTER THAN *YOU'LL* EVER KNOW HER, SONNY BOY!

HEY, I DON'T HAVE TO TAKE THIS SORT OF CRAP FROM SOME *STUPID FROG!!*
FROG?

KSSHHH

FOOL. DON'T YOU *RECOGNIZE* MY VOICE... THE VOICE IN YOUR *NIGHT-MARE...?*
I'M HERE TO GIVE YOU YOUR NEW BODY.

AIEEEE
N-N-NIGHT-MARE?! N-N-NEW BODY?!
KEIICHI ?!
BUT HOW?!
THE BARRIER COULDN'T HAVE BEEN THAT EASY TO BREAK THROUGH!
HEH HEH HEH... BUT YOU WERE A BIT CARELESS WHEN YOU BUILT IT...
...MY DEAR BELL-DANDY.
MARA!!

KEIICHI!!!
NO!!
OH, KEIICHI, I'M *SO* SORRY! THIS IS ALL *MY* FAULT!
NOT THE *FROG*. THE *NEWT* !!
oops

GIVE HIM BACK HIS REAL FORM *NOW*, MARA!!
AS A GODDESS FIRST-CLASS, I *COMMAND* YOU!
NOW, YOU KNOW BETTER THAN THAT.
I'M A ***DEMON*** FIRST-CLASS. I DON'T HAVE TO TAKE ORDERS FROM YOU.
HAVE FUN SNUGGLING UP WITH YOUR *DARLING*, DEAR!
HI, GUYS!
?

NOT THE FROG. THE NEWT!

ALTHOUGH I GUESS HE'S A *LIZARD* NOW...

I HAVE TO ADMIT THIS IS PRETTY CRUEL...EVEN BY *MARA'S* STANDARDS!!

WHAT?! MARA'S HERE?!

HEY, WHAT'S UP?

UM...

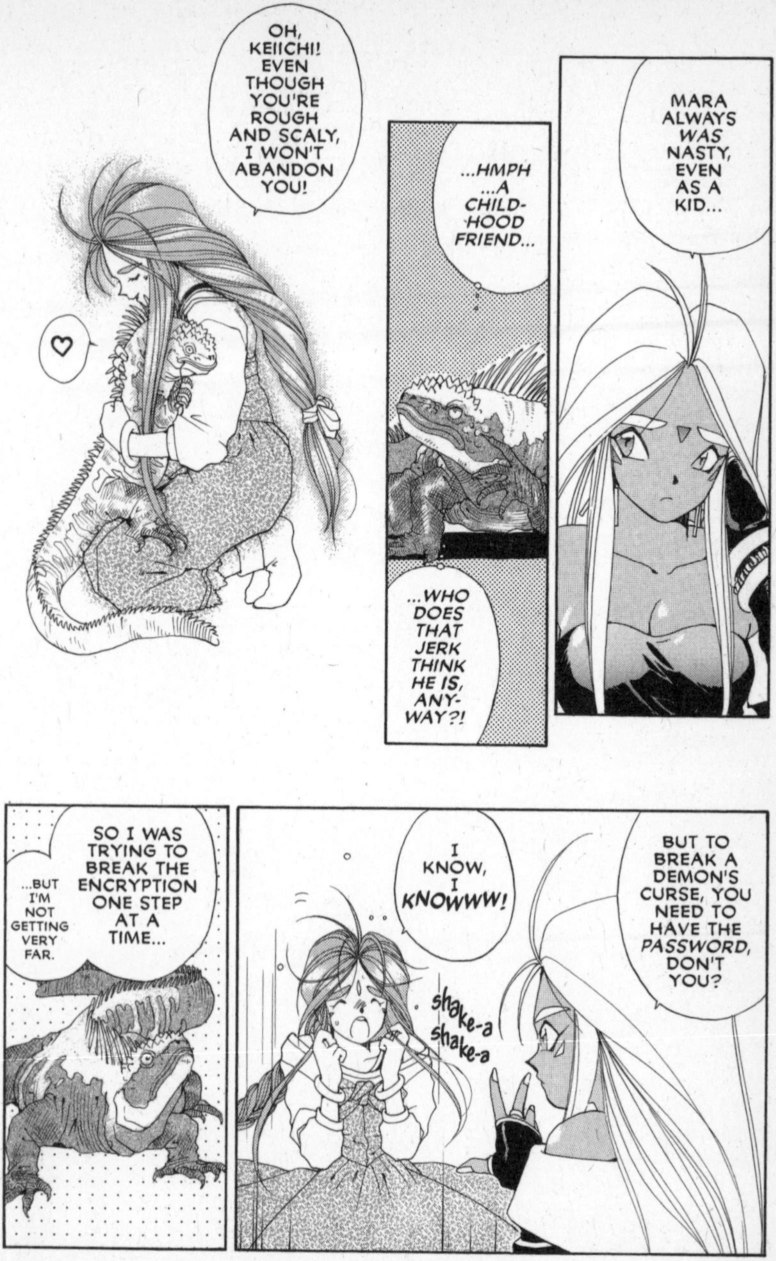

MARA ALWAYS *WAS* NASTY, EVEN AS A KID...

...HMPH ...A CHILD-HOOD FRIEND...

...WHO DOES THAT JERK THINK HE IS, ANY-WAY?!

OH, KEIICHI! EVEN THOUGH YOU'RE ROUGH AND SCALY, I WON'T ABANDON YOU!

♡

BUT TO BREAK A DEMON'S CURSE, YOU NEED TO HAVE THE *PASSWORD*, DON'T YOU?
I KNOW, I ***KNOWWW!***
shake-a
shake-a

SO I WAS TRYING TO BREAK THE ENCRYPTION ONE STEP AT A TIME...
...BUT I'M NOT GETTING VERY FAR.

POOF
RIGHT! GETTING CLOSER!
AND NOW!
POOF
OKAY!
POOF
HERE, SIS, LET *URD* FINISH THE JOB!
HEY, *HEY!!*
POOF

WE'LL JUST HAVE TO GET *MARA* TO BREAK THE SPELL.

NEVER MIND. YOU'RE RIGHT...WE WON'T GET ANYWHERE WITHOUT THE PASSWORD ANYWAY.
ER... SORRY.

...BUT HOW ARE WE GOING TO GET SOMEONE LIKE MARA TO DO *THAT...?*

THE *CATALYST* !!

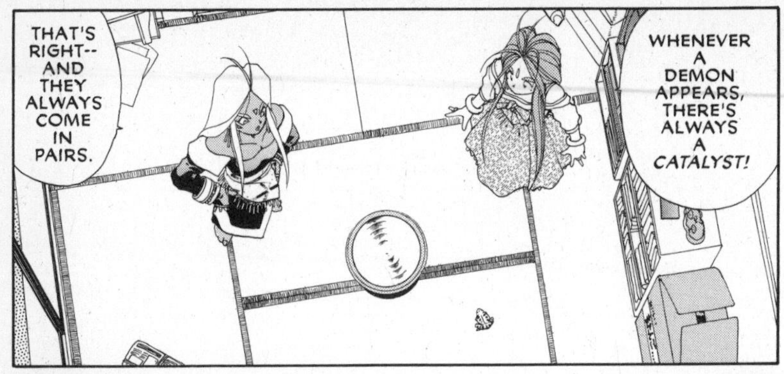
WHENEVER A DEMON APPEARS, THERE'S ALWAYS A *CATALYST!*
THAT'S RIGHT-- AND THEY ALWAYS COME IN PAIRS.

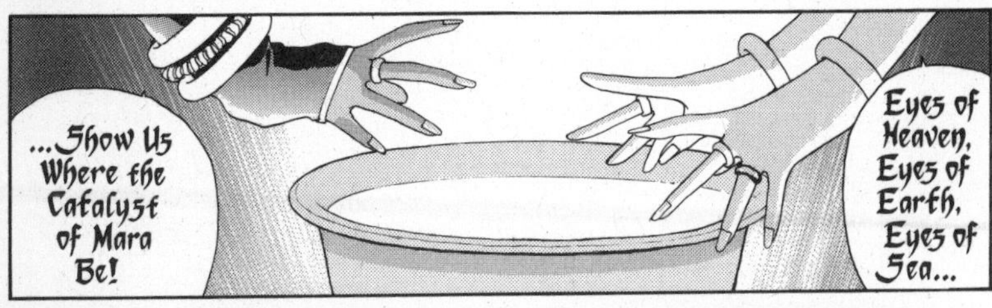
Eyes of Heaven, Eyes of Earth, Eyes of Sea...
...Show Us Where the Catalyst of Mara Be!

WELL ...?
OH!

IT'S CLOSE... AND IT'S GETTING ***CLOSER!***

THAT'S *IT!!*

huh?

SKKRUNK

YO, MORI-SATO!

YOU GOTS A *CD* PLAYER?

GUESS I'D BETTER LOOK FOR A PLACE TO STAY...

tap

....

...AH ...*BELL-DANDY.*

...MARA!
GIVE KEIICHI BACK HIS NATURAL FORM THIS *INSTANT!!*

...OH ...OKAY.
I MEAN, **NO.**

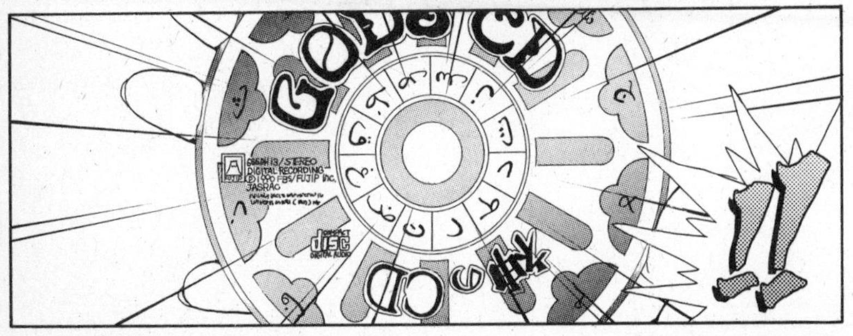

NO!

ONE FOR DEMONS... ONE FOR GODS!!
THAT'S RIGHT, MARA! IT'S A DOUBLE DISC SET!
THE CD OF THE GODS...!!
AND IT'S CERTAINLY POWERFUL ENOUGH TO BIND YOU!!

NO! WAIT!!
WHY?!
WHY IS A *GODDESS* LIKE YOU PLAYING SERVANT TO A MERE *HUMAN?!*
YOU CAN BREAK YOUR CONTRACT WITH HIM ANYTIME YOU *WANT!!*
I'M NOT *HERE* JUST BECAUSE OF A *CONTRACT!*
I'M ALSO HERE OF MY OWN *FREE WILL!!*

HRRGH!

OKAY!
OKAY!! I'LL TELL YOU THE PASS-WORD!!

...WHICH DIDN'T RETURN KEIICHI'S CLOTHES...
Kyaa!
gasp!

...NOR GET RID OF THE PERSON WHO HAD CAUSED ALL THE TROUBLE.
DAMN... NOW I *REALLY* GOTTA FIND A PLACE.
HEY, BUDDY... WANT SOME O' THIS BURGER I FOUND?

CHAPTER 27

Mara's Counterattack

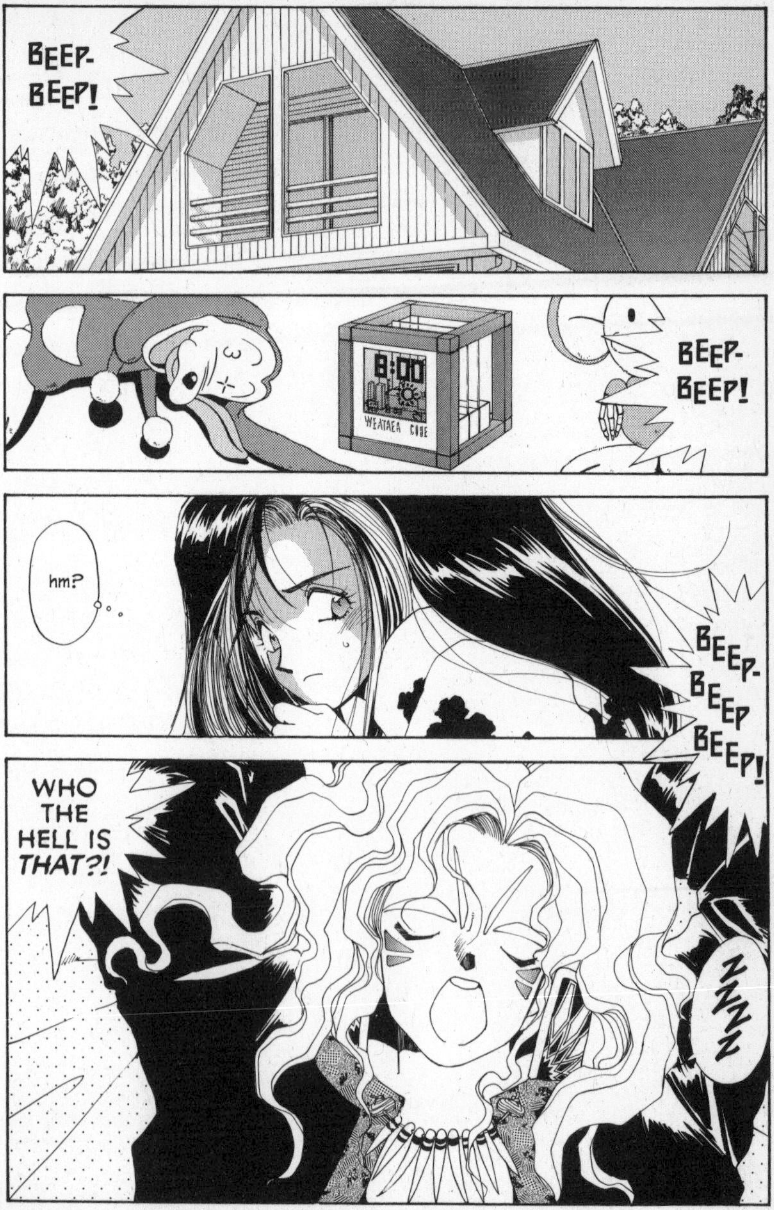

hm?

BEEP-BEEP BEEP BEEP!

WHO THE HELL IS *THAT?!*

ZZZZ

WHAT HAPPENED LAST...
huh?
beep beep
NOW, JUST CALM DOWN, SAYOKO.
huh ?!
I CAN'T REMEMBER! FROM THE TIME I LEFT SCHOOL YESTERDAY, MY MIND'S A COMPLETE BLANK!!
THAT'S CRAZY! EVEN IF I DID GET TOTALLY SLOSHED, I SHOULD AT LEAST REMEMBER WHAT HAPPENED BEFORE I STARTED DRINKING!!
LET'S SEE... AFTER MY LAST CLASS...
I GOT IN MY CAR...
...AND THEN...
...AND THEN... AND THEN WHAT HAPPENED?
fwip fwap

THAT'S RIGHT! I BOUGHT A CD YESTERDAY!
NOW, IF I CAN ONLY FIND...
blink!
hmmmm...
snff
huh?
青炒老醜
STEREO
武江人民公社
HERE IT IS!!

CD?

DID YOU SAY A CD?!
hahh
hahh
!!

uh... what?
DEMON'S CD

EEEEKK!!

THE DEMONS CD AND GODS CD FORM AN INSEPARABLE PAIR.
THEY'RE A 2-CD SET, YOU KNOW... NOT AVAILABLE ON LP OR CASSETTE.
OH, YES.
Y- Y-YOU MEAN THAT DEMON'S STILL AROUND?!
BUT I CAN'T LET MARA HAVE THE GODS CD-- THAT'S MY TRUMP CARD.
WITHOUT BOTH OF THEM, MARA CAN'T LEAVE.
SO HE'S GONNA HANG AROUND HERE FOREVER?!
...IF ONLY THE DEMON WOULD DECIDE TO LEAVE OF ITS OWN ACCORD...
but, no.

WHAT ABOUT USING THE *GODS CD...*
...TO *SEAL MARA UP?*

YEAH! DO IT! DO IT!
LET'S SEE HOW A DEMON LIKES A TASTE OF ITS OWN MEDICINE!
AND OTHER CLICHÉS!
THE IDIOT TURNED ME INTO A NEWT... AND A *FROG,* TOO!

ACTUALLY, IDIOT, *MARA* TURNED YOU INTO THE NEWT.
I TURNED YOU INTO THE FROG.
yeah... right.

NO, NO, WE JUST *CAN'T.*
why not?
IF I SEAL MARA UP, SHE'LL BE TRAPPED FOR *500 YEARS.*
IT SEEMS TOO CRUEL... EVEN FOR A DEMON.

BUT MARA'S BOUND TO COME FOR THE CD...
...SOONER OR LATER.
EEK! HELP!
HEY. WAIT. HEY!
GET OUT OF HERE!!
WHO ARE YOU? I'VE NEVER SEEN YOU BEFORE!!
LAY OFF! THE NAME'S--
trip!

um...
AND YOUR EEEEEVIL PSYCHIC EMANATIONS CALLED ME!
--THE NAME'S MARA... DEMON FIRST CLASS!!
YOU WANT TO GET RID OF BELLDANDY, DON'T YOU?
SO DON'T PLAY THE GOOD GIRL.
UH-OH!
JUST HOW POWERFUL ARE THOSE EMANATIONS?!
BELL-DANDY...?!

BELL-DANDY?!

EEEEK!!

LEMME GET THIS STRAIGHT...

...YOU'LL HELP *ME* GET BELLDANDY OUT OF THE PICTURE... IS THAT RIGHT?
ER, YEAH...

HOW'D THIS "MARA" KNOW ABOUT ME AND BELL-DANDY, ANYWAY?

...BUT WHO CARES, AS LONG AS A DEMON'S AS GOOD AS ITS WORD?

OKAY, YOU'RE *ON!*

NOW... WHAT DO I OWE YOU IN RETURN? MY SOUL? SOMETHING LIKE THAT?

Close O Guardian Seal... Till Next You Hear My Command...
And May Any Who Touch Thee... Be Seized By the Wrath of Heaven!

DEMON'S CD
蟻せんべい

phew
...BUT WHY PUT A SEAL ON THE *GODS* CD?

IT'S LIKE PUTTING AN EMERGENCY SWITCH BEHIND GLASS...
...THIS WAY I'M NOT SO TEMPTED TO SIMPLY *USE* IT.

AWW, YOU DON'T HAVE TO GO TO ALL THAT *TROUBLE!*

JUST LEAVE EVERYTHING TO YOUR BIG SIS *URD!*

huh?

URD

YOU'VE GOT TO THINK OF THE *ENVIRONMENT* BEFORE YOU DUMP HORRIBLE, TOXIC THINGS DOWN THE DRAIN!
RIGHT, URD?
UH... *YEAH!*
RIGHT... EVERYONE'S GOT A POINT...

THE SINK! QUICK!
glub glub
HEY!!
I WORKED **HARD** ON THAT!

SHAME ON YOU, KEIICHI!

tock tick

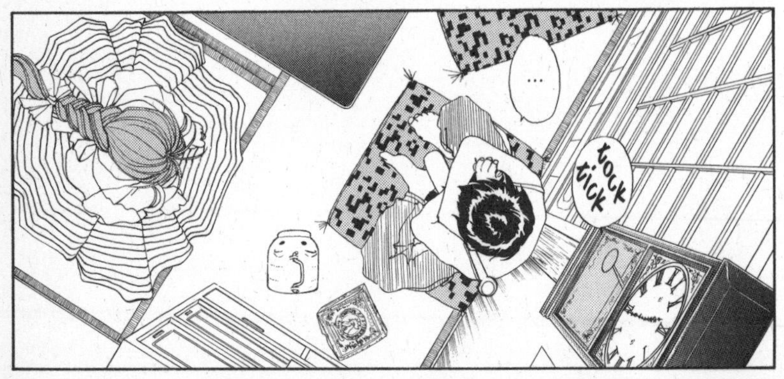
...
tock tick

tick
tock

I'VE GOT MY BASEBALL BAT...
...I'M READY.

MARA'S COM-ING...
...THE DISTURB-ANCE IS GETTING STRONGER! WE *MUST* BE VIGILANT!

ZZZZZZ

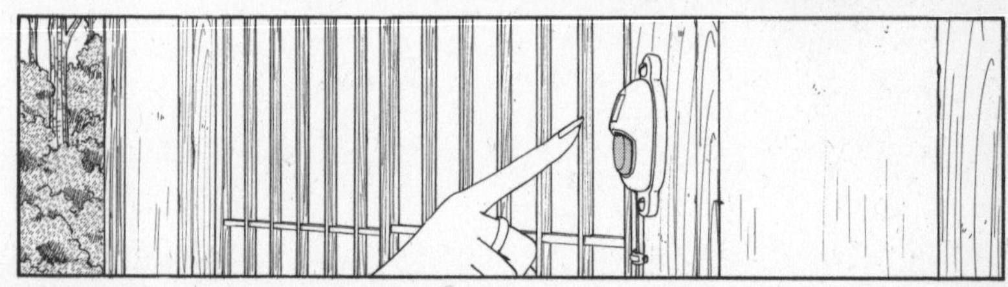

....it's sayoko.

OH, HI...

KILL!! KILL!!

URD MAGIC

WHAT'D SHE COME AROUND FOR, ANYWAY?
OH, THAT'S OKAY-- DON'T EVEN *WORRY* ABOUT IT!
psycho witch!!
I'M *SO* SORRY! WE WERE EXPECTING... *uh...* *SOME-ONE ELSE!*
Drink Coca-Cola

EEEEKK!!
WHAT NOW?
I'M AFRAID IT MAY BE...
...LET'S SEE... SUPPOSED TO BE IN A SEALED BOX LABELLED ANT CRACKERS...
shff
A-HA!!
I'M STUCK! I CAN'T MOVE!!
SO! TRYING TO SWIPE OUR ANT CRACKERS, EH? WHY DIDN'T YOU JUST ASK?
I DON'T CARE ABOUT YOUR STUPID ANT CRACKERS!

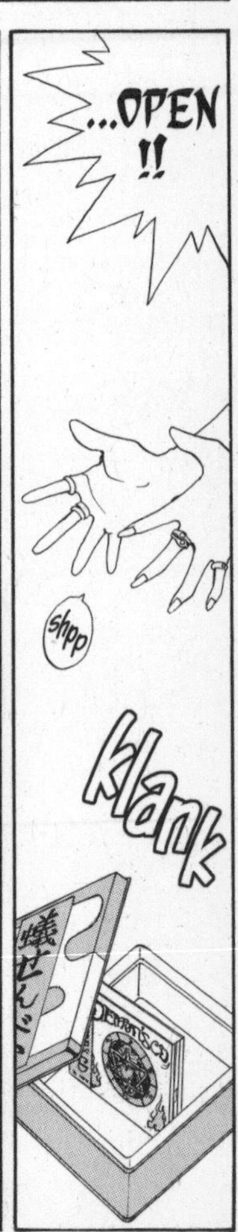

HAR-DEE HAR HAR *HAR!* THANKS FOR THE *CD*, CHUMPS!!

NOW I'M FREE! **FREE!**

hee-hee-hee!

thmp

S-SOME-THING'S *PULLING* ME *DOWN* ...?!
TH-THE *GODS CD?!* B-BUT--
--*HOW* DID YOU--?!

FWHAM!

IF THAT'S THE GODS CD, THEN WHAT'S IN HERE...?

KSSShhh

....

Golden Reggae Hits

WARNINGS ON THE USE OF THIS CD:

WELL...IT SEEMED A SHAME TO JUST SEAL IT UP LIKE THAT, SO I PUT IN A SUBSTITUTE...

LOOK, MARA, PLEASE...
...WON'T YOU JUST GO HOME NOW?

HAH! DON'T WASTE YOUR BREATH, DEAR! AFTER ALL--
--I'VE GOT THE OTHER ONE!!
ZRAK
!!
SKSSHHH

MARA, IF WE KEEP THIS UP, EVERYONE WILL GET CAUGHT IN THE VORTEX!!

GBLORP

BLUBB BLUBB

....

IS THAT WHAT YOU WANT?!

HMM...

WAIT! BELL-DANDY! WHAT ARE YOU *DOING?!*

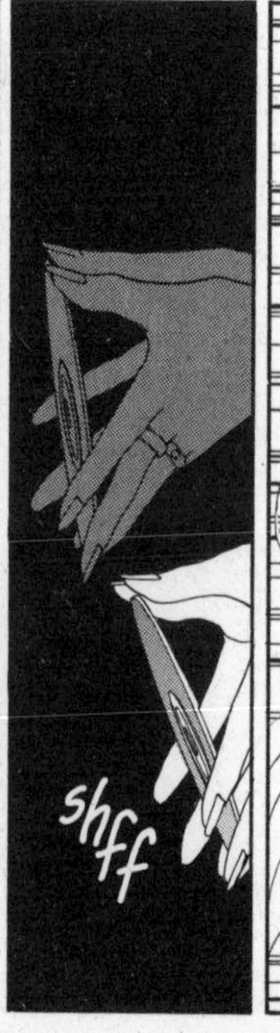
shff

EVEN IF I'M SEALED IN...THE INTERACTION WITH THE **GODS CD** MAY LET ME BREAK FREE...

I NEVER EXPECTED THINGS TO GO *THIS* FAR--
--BUT THAT'S JUST TOO BAD. I HAVE MY OWN JOB TO DO.
WAIT!! STOP!!
BLORP BLORP
H-*HEY!* WHAT'S THAT HORRIBLE, TOXIC *THING* DOWN THERE?!
KANGG
GLURGGLE

GBLOOSH
!!
Shlooopp
gulp
IT... *IT...*
DON'T CALL IT AN "IT"... I *MADE...* *er, IT!*
C'MON, GIVE IT BACK! ***PLEEEASE!!***
brr rrrpppp
I THINK YOU'RE GONNA HAFTA WAIT TILL IT TAKES A CRAP.
NOW, KEIICHI... DO YOU SEE WHAT HAPPENS WHEN YOU DUMP THINGS DOWN THE DRAIN?
OKAY... NOW I'VE ***TOTALLY*** LOST THE POINT.

CHAPTER 28
Balance-Ball Amour

AW, IT'S TOO *NICE* A DAY TO STAY INSIDE, KEIICHI! C'MON! YOU TWO GO OUT AND HAVE SOME *FUN!*
HEY! GIVE IT *BACK!!*
THAT HOME-WORK'S DUE *TOMORROW!*
IF YOU SPEND ALL YOUR TIME INDOORS, YOU'LL TURN (or around here, maybe *be turned*) INTO A *MUSHROOM,* KIDDO!
DON'T TRY ANY *TRICKS!*
poof
poof
poof

STOP IT RIGHT NOW!!

NOW, URD-- KEIICHI COULDN'T GET ANY OF HIS SCHOOLWORK DONE DURING THAT TROUBLE WITH MARA!!
RIGHT NOW!!
RIGHT NOW!!

OH... WAIT... COULD YOU HEAR THAT?

NEVER MIND! KEIICHI, MAYBE WE SHOULD GO OUT!

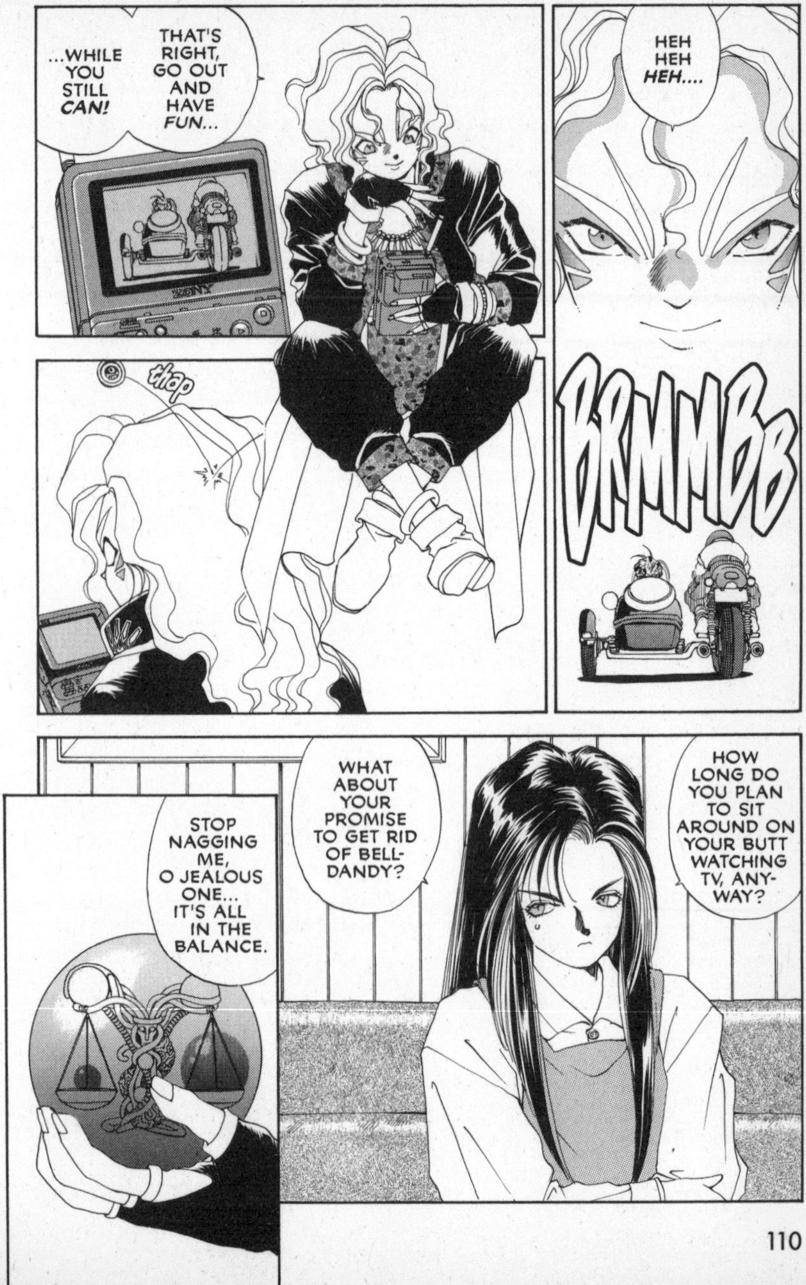

THAT'S RIGHT, GO OUT AND HAVE *FUN*...
...WHILE YOU STILL *CAN!*
HEH HEH *HEH*....
thap
BRMMBB

WHAT ABOUT YOUR PROMISE TO GET RID OF BELL-DANDY?
HOW LONG DO YOU PLAN TO SIT AROUND ON YOUR BUTT WATCHING TV, ANY-WAY?
STOP NAGGING ME, O JEALOUS ONE... IT'S ALL IN THE BALANCE.

WHAT'S *THAT?*
LOOKS LIKE A CRYSTAL BALL...
INDEED! BUT *THIS* ONE MEASURES THE BALANCE OF KEIICHI'S ***HEART.***
AND WHEN SOMEONE'S HEART IS IN THE BALANCE, IT CAN BE TIPPED EITHER WAY.
THEREFORE A LITTLE *PUSH*...AND KEIICHI'S HEART SHALL BECOME ***YOURS.***
DON'T WASTE YOUR TIME.
MY GOAL IS TO GET RID OF ***BELL-DANDY...*** THAT'S ALL.
KEIICHI'S JUST A MEANS TO THAT END.
INDEED HE IS, MY DEAR.

NOVA

JUST SMELL THAT FRESH AIR!!
AREN'T YOU GLAD WE WENT OUT?

I KNOW YOU CAN'T AFFORD TO NEGLECT YOUR HOMEWORK *TOO* MUCH, SO WHEN YOU DO...

...YOU'VE GOT TO MAKE THE *MOST* OF IT!
right?

YEAH... I GUESS...
ALL RIGHT, THEN! I WON'T EVEN ***THINK*** ABOUT HOMEWORK UNTIL WE GET BACK!

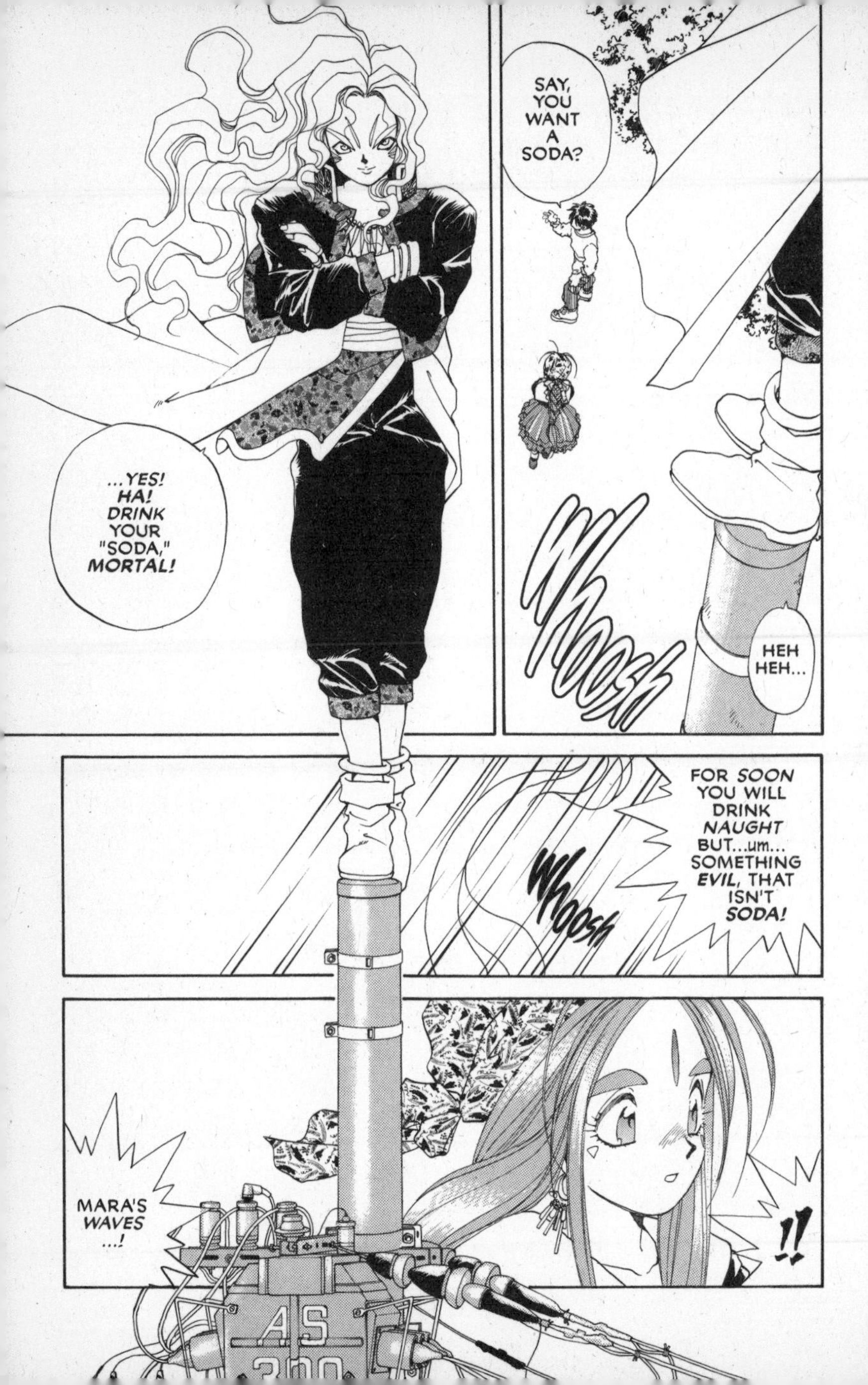
...YES! HA! DRINK YOUR "SODA," MORTAL!
SAY, YOU WANT A SODA?
WHOOSH
HEH HEH...
FOR SOON YOU WILL DRINK NAUGHT BUT...um... SOMETHING EVIL, THAT ISN'T SODA!
WHOOSH
MARA'S WAVES ...!
!!
AS

Big Rig Awake...

A... Loser's Life to TAKE!

rrrmmm

MUST BE OUT OF ORDER...

HEY, WHAT'S *WRONG* WITH THIS STUPID MACHINE ?!

IT WON'T GIVE ME MY *MONEY* BACK, EITHER!

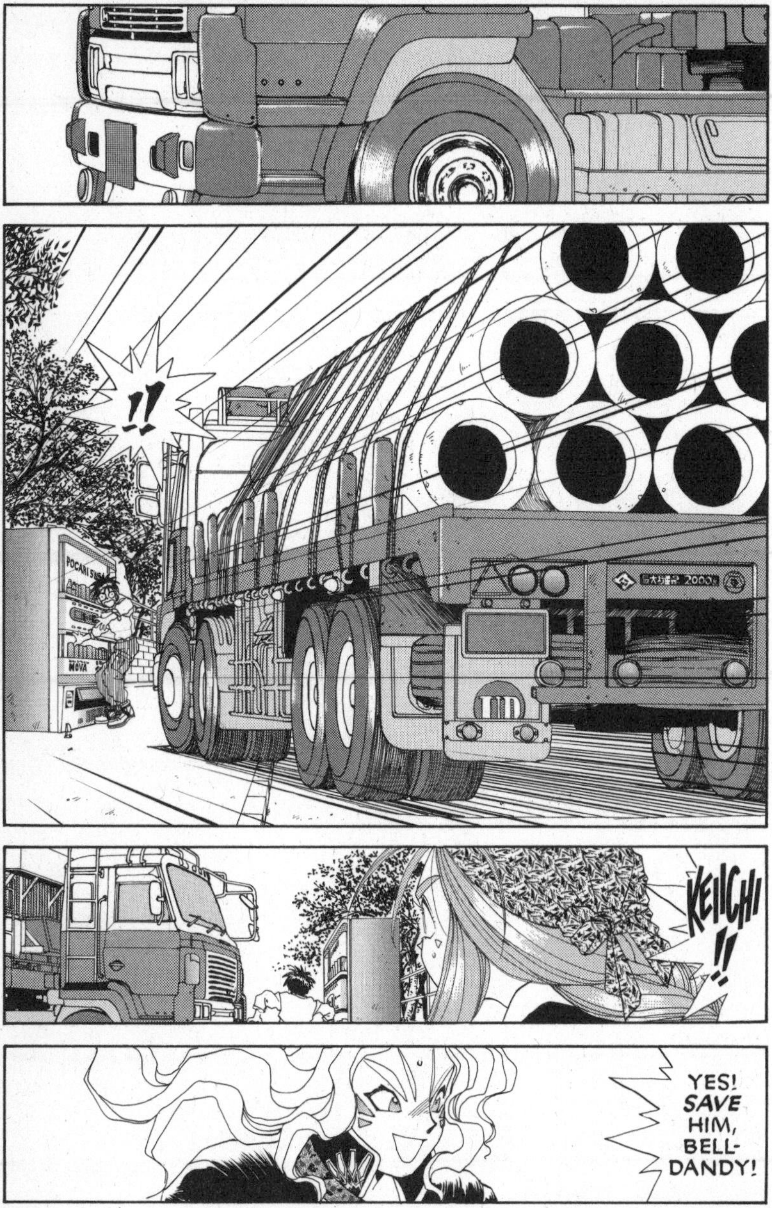

!!

KEIICHI !!

YES! *SAVE* HIM, BELL-DANDY!

FORGIVE ME, KEIICHI... I MUST KNOCK YOU CLEAR WITH*...
VVmmmmm
ZAPP
VRNCH
*A SPHERE OF PURE ENERGY!

!!
OW
OW...
hey...
...WHY AM I STILL ALIVE?

AND HOW CAN I STAY THAT WAY?!

Posts and Lanterns Rise from Street... Plant Thyself As a Gate of Steel!

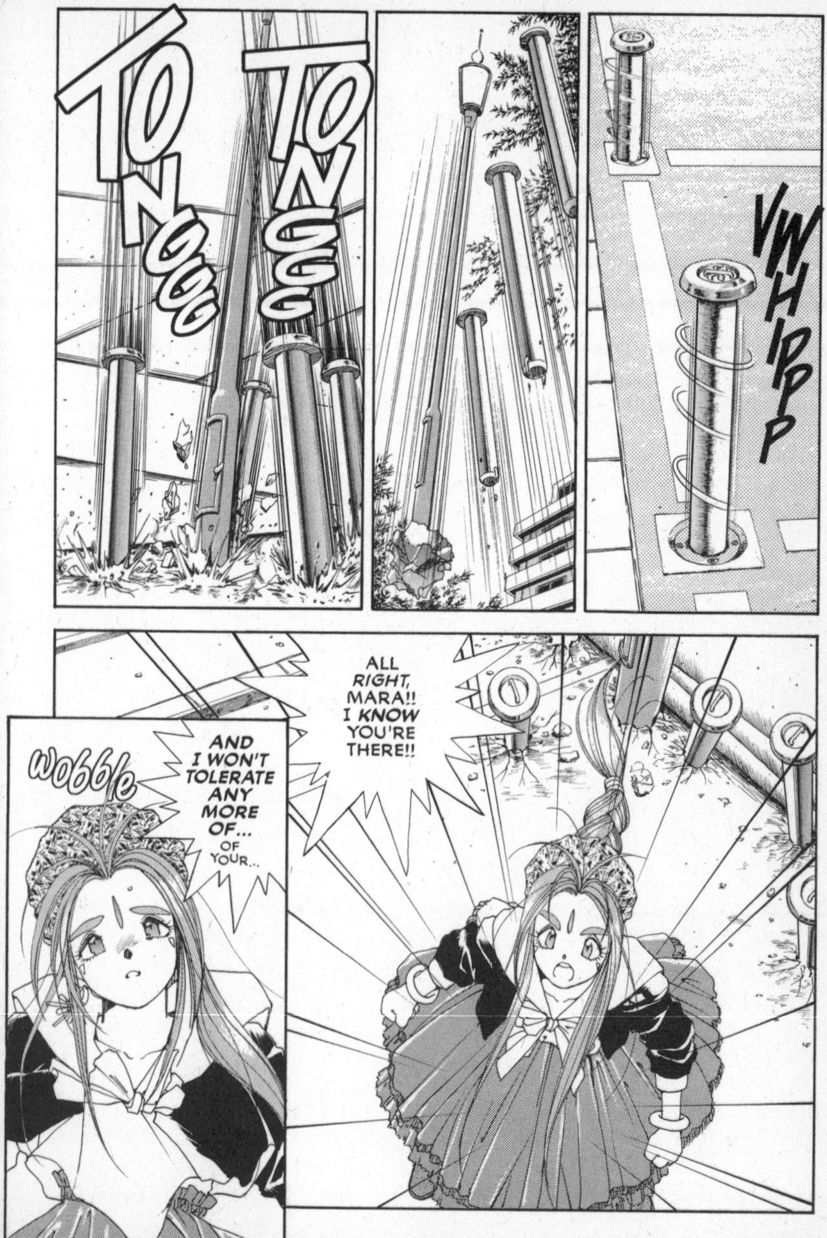

TONGGG
TONGGG
VWHIPPP
ALL RIGHT, MARA!! I KNOW YOU'RE THERE!!
AND I WON'T TOLERATE ANY MORE OF... OF YOUR...
wobble

BELL!

...AWFUL... behav...

HMMM... IT SEEMS YOU USED UP ALL YOUR *STRENGTH*...
...IT DIDN'T TAKE *LONG*, DID IT?

MY *ANKLE!*

SPLORSH

YOU WERE LOOKING AFTER ME!

I'M SORRY... IT'S ALL *MY* FAULT!

PARKING TICKET

DAMN YOU, MARA !!

HEY! I ONLY DID THE *TRUCK* STUFF!
MAYBE HE'S JUST ONE OF THOSE SUCKERS WHO WAS BORN UNDER A BAD SIGN.

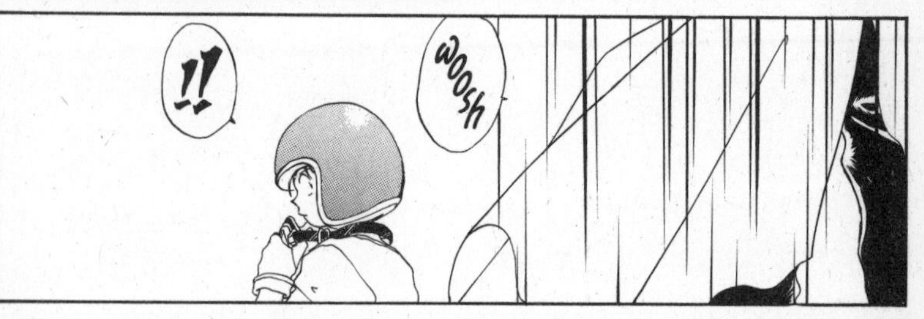
WOOSH
!!

YES...
...IT CERTAINLY *IS* YOUR FAULT, KEIICHI.

SHUT UP, YOU!
IT'S ONLY BECAUSE *YOU'RE* CAUSING ALL THE TROUBLE!
ESPECIALLY THAT *PARKING TICKET*... THAT WAS EVIL!
AH, BUT I *DO* HAVE THE RIGHT.
YOU SEE...

BELL-DANDY'S MY *FIANCÉE...*

FIANCÉ?!

NO. NOT "FIANCÉ" "FIANCÉE."
FEMI-NINE.
n-no...

YOUR HEART SHALL TILT! ...YOU SHALL BE IN MY POWER!
SOON YOU SHALL HAVE NO CHOICE BUT TO DO MY BIDDING!

16 17 18 19 20
23 24 25 26 27
30 31
BACK SO SOON?
NOT ONLY ARE PEOPLE SICK, BUT...
...SHE USED UP ALL HER POWERS AGAIN ?!
WHAT HAP-PENED, KEIICHI?
YOU DON'T WANNA KNOW...

YOU DIDN'T TAKE ADVANTAGE OF HER, DID YOU?
NO...
remorse
guilt

EDEN
...OKAY, KEIICHI! THIS POTION SHOULD FIX HER UP...

YO! KEIICHI ...?
WHERE'D HE GO...?
!!

poof
poof
poof
LISTEN TO *THIS* FIRST.
AND I'M NOT ABOUT TO LOSE TO A MERE DEMON LIKE *YOU*!
fssshhhh
HO HO HO! I WASN'T BORN *YESTERDAY*, MARA!!
poof
poof

THE... THE HEAD-PHONES ...!
tmp
WHOOOSH
!!
klik
THAT... THAT SOUND ...!!!
HE'S ABOUT TO TIP TO ONE SIDE.
fzzzzmm
IT'LL BE ANY TIME NOW.

SOON! SOON!
NYA HA HA!
....
WHAT'S UP, KEIICHI?
YOU LOOK LIKE YOU COULD USE SOME-ONE TO TALK TO.
SAYOKO ...?

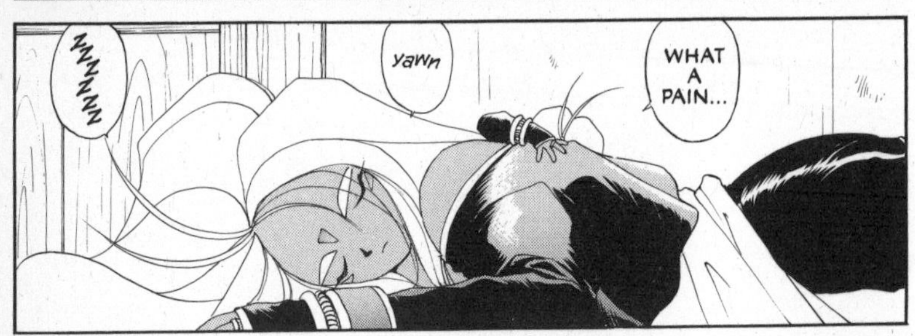

IT'S A GOOD THING I LEFT A SPARE *MINI-URD* LOOSE.

THE *BIG* ME WILL BE OUT FOR A WHILE!

ENKA MUSIC.

ALWAYS BORES ME TO *SLEEP!*

Come to me with your muscle-ness...

MARA *KNEW* THE EFFECT IT WOULD HAVE ON ME...

...IT'S DEMONIC!

OF COURSE... SHE *IS* A DEMON...

I'VE GOT TO WAKE *BELL-DANDY!*

hmm...
...I SEE.

BUT, YOU KNOW...
IT SOUNDS LIKE BELLDANDY HELPS YOU OUT BY HER OWN CHOICE.
SO WHY FEEL GUILTY OVER THAT, KEIICHI?!

BUT NOW YOU FIND OUT SHE'S ENGAGED TO SOMEONE ELSE--SOUNDS LIKE SOME KIND OF CHEESY SOAP OPERA!
WHY DON'T YOU GO OUT WITH ME, HUH? I'M NOT THE POSSESSIVE TYPE. YOU'LL ALWAYS BE FREE.

YOU'RE A REAL SWEET-HEART, SAYOKO.

THANKS FOR TRYING TO MAKE ME FEEL BETTER.
UH... I WAS SERIOUS, Y'KNOW...

EXCELLENT, MY DEAR!

...THERE YOU GO, KEIICHI.... THERE YOU...
NOW, IF I FOCUS MY ENERGY... AND INCREASE HER CHARISMA JUST A BIT MORE...

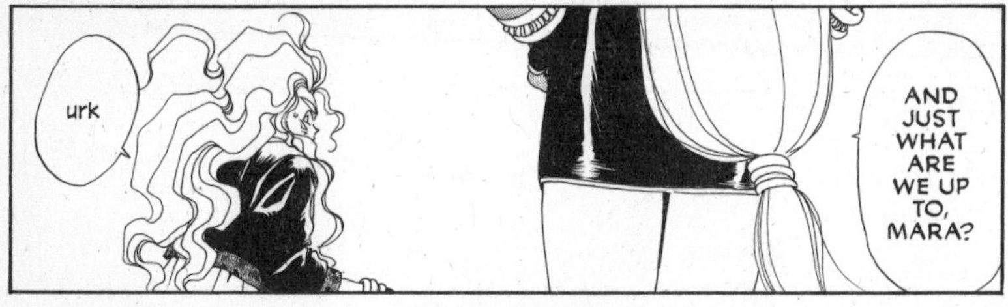
AND JUST WHAT ARE WE UP TO, MARA?
urk
I MEAN... IF YOU NO LONGER WANT ME...
TH-THEN I GUESS I WON'T BE NEEDED HERE ANYMORE, KEIICHI.
MAYBE I *SHOULD* SWITCH TO YOU... HUH, SAYOKO.
really?

...I HAVE NO CHOICE BUT TO RETURN HOME.
TH... THANKS FOR THE LOVELY TIME... KEIICHI!
YEAH, SURE. WE DON'T WANT TO GET TOO COMMITTED, RIGHT?
NO!!
IT WAS FUN WHILE IT LASTED.
NO! NO!! STOP!!!

DON'T GO, BELL-DANDY!
THAT WASN'T ME SAYING THAT!
STOP!! I DIDN'T MEAN IT!!!
!!
C'MON, SIS.
DOES THAT EVEN SOUND LIKE KEIIICHI?
...HE WAS POSSESSED THROUGH THIS BALANCE SPHERE, BY...
...SHOW YOUR-SELF, MARA.

CURSES !!

SHE CAST THE *HEADPHONES OF HARD ROCK* UPON ME! I'M *REVEALED!*

IT'S DEMONIC!

THAT'S RIGHT... HARD ROCK *IS* DEMONIC...

fwish

BUT IF YOU'RE MARA'S FIANCÉE...

MARA'S *FIANCÉE* ?!!

IS *THAT* WHAT SHE TOLD YOU?!

chuckle! chortle!

"she"?

NO, MARA'S NOT MY FIANCÉE.

I'VE BEEN MEANING TO TELL YOU THIS, BUT... MARA'S A *WOMAN.*

HE DIDN'T KNOW! HE DIDN'T KNOW!

W-WHAT ?!

LOOK... STOP YOUR SINFUL GYRATING TO THE BEAT, OR I'M OUT OF HERE.

CAN'T STOP... *THE MUSIC!*

dance!

dance!

CHAPTER 29

The Worst Day of a Demon

THE ~~DEMON~~ DEMONNESS MARA, WHO HAD SHOWN UP TO TROUBLE BELLDANDY...
...AIN'T BEEN SEEN IN THESE PARTS FOR QUITE A WHILE.

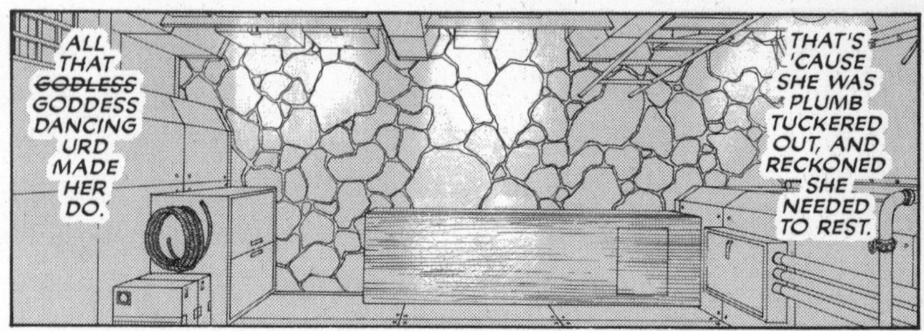
THAT'S 'CAUSE SHE WAS PLUMB TUCKERED OUT, AND RECKONED SHE NEEDED TO REST.
ALL THAT ~~GODLESS~~ GODDESS DANCING URD MADE HER DO.

KREEEK

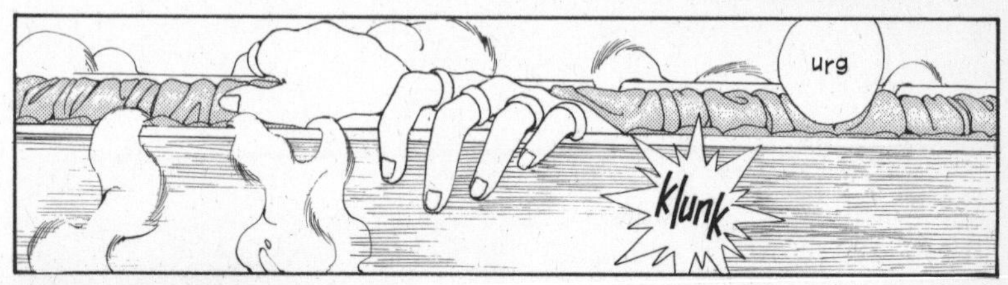
urg
klunk

hahh
hahh

yaaawn
fwap

HMPH!
THESE JAPANESE COFFINS ARE SURE SHORT ON *FRILLS!*

nngg!
THAT DAMNED URD REALLY DID A NUMBER ON ME. I SLEPT LIKE AN UNHOLY LOG.
FZZRAKK
I WONDER WHAT DAY IT IS HERE ON EARTH, ANYWAY?

SSSSSSHHHHHH
WELL, IT DOESN'T MATTER FOR *YOU,* KEIICHI--
--BECAUSE *EVERY* DAY'S GOING TO BE A DAY IN *HELL* WHILE *I'M* AROUND!

2
1月 水
"Make every day your best day!"
BOY! THIS IS A *HECK* OF A DAY!
IT'S NICE TO HAVE THE NEW YEAR'S HOLIDAYS BE SO QUIET AND RELAXING!
AS OPPOSED TO THE FREEZING TORMENT I ENDURED *LAST* YEAR...
AND WE HAVEN'T HEARD FROM MARA FOR QUITE A WHILE, HAVE WE?
OKAY, EVERYBODY-- HOW ABOUT A NEW YEAR'S GAME OF CARDS?!
WHATEVER IT SAYS ON THE CARD YOU PICK COMES TRUE...
fwipppp
YEAH, RIGHT... WE'VE ALREADY BEEN THROUGH THAT.
AND *ONCE* IS ENOUGH!
NO, NO... THAT WAS A *DIFFERENT* GAME!

HMM... WHAT'S KEEPING MEGUMI? SHE'S LATE!
OH, IS YOUR SISTER COMING OVER TODAY?
I DUNNO WHY I'M GOING TO ALL THIS TROUBLE FOR MY DUMB BROTHER...
WHAT'S HE NEED A GOOD-LUCK CHARM FOR ANYWAY? I MEAN...
...HE ALREADY *LIVES* IN A TEMPLE!
BESIDES, IT'S *COLD* RIDING AROUND ON THIS BIKE.
BRMMMR
BEING IN A *CAR* WOULD BE NICE...
chatter chatter

HEH-HEH-HEH!
SO, LITTLE BRAT! YOU'RE KEIICHI'S SISTER, EH?
IT SHALL BE JUST AS YOU WISH!
YOUR *BEING*... IN A CAR!

NYA-HA-HA!! DON'T FEEL *TOO* BAD, KID!!
KEIICHI AND *ALL* HIS FRIENDS WILL BE GETTING THE *SAME TREATMENT!!*
HMM... WHAT SHOULD I TURN KEIICHI INTO?
A TRICYCLE? IT HAS TO BE SOMETHING THAT *ROLLS*...
...A-HA! *TOILET PAPER!*
step
WHA--?!
ZZRAKKK

WOBBLING... MUST GRAB ONTO...

ZZZKKKK

I TOUCHED THE TEMPLE! OH, THIS SMARTS!

OW OW OW

toink

I...I STEPPED ON A HAMAYA... ARROW OF GOOD LUCK!

A PO-- A PO--
JEEZ, SHE'S LIKE, AN HOUR LATE!
HAW! HAW!
I'LL COME WITH YOU.
I'M GONNA GO TAKE A LOOK DOWN THE STREET.

--A PORSCHE 356 SPEEDSTER !!!
THIS--
--COULD IT BE?!
MEGUMI? WHERE ARE YOU?
RIGHT HERE !!
KEI-chaaaan!
HUH?

DON'T YOU *GET* IT?

WOW!! LIKE KNIGHT RIDER!

THE *CAR*, STUPID!! THE *CAR* IS ME!!

geez!

SLAM

SLAM

I CANNOT FREE HER... BUT LET HER FORM HAVE MOTION!

YES! I CAN SEE MEGUMI'S SPIRIT EMANATING FROM THE CARBURETOR!!!

megumi's spirit

(EMANATING FROM THE CARBURETOR)

UNTERMBOCANICA

YOUR OWN SISTER TURNS INTO A *CAR*, AND *THAT'S* ALL YOU CAN SAY?!

ER...

...I GOTTA HAND IT TO YA, SIS, YOU'RE A LOT BETTER LOOKING THAN THE LAST TIME I SAW YOU.

'CAUSE WATCH ME PULL THESE *DONUTS*! THESE ARE *DREAM* *DONUTS*!

SKREEEEEEE

A *DREAM*!! THIS HAS TO BE A *DREAM*!

MARA?! DID YOU TURN MY SISTER INTO A *PORSCHE* 356?!
UM.
HEAD HURTS.
OH--!
HI. DO I KNOW YOU?
huh?!
huh?!
huh?!
IT LOOKS LIKE SHE STEPPED ON THIS *HAMAYA*...

...AND THEN TOUCHED THE *TEMPLE*... THUS A CURRENT OF ***KARMIC SHOCK*** FLOWED THROUGH HER.
HUH-- I DIDN'T KNOW GOOD LUCK CHARMS WERE SUCH A PROBLEM FOR MARA.

LET'S TEST HER ON MY LOTTO TICKET!
OWW! MY HEAD!!
great!
URD! DON'T BE MEAN!

PLEASE... FORGIVE ME.
I SEEM TO HAVE CAUSED YOU NICE PEOPLE A GREAT DEAL OF TROUBLE.

SHE'S A LOT NICER WITHOUT HER *MEMORY*... WHY DON'T WE JUST LEAVE HER THE WAY SHE IS?
UNFORTU-NATELY, WE CAN'T.
WHY NOT?

SO, IF MARA DOESN'T GET HER MEMORY BACK--
--MEGUMI WILL BE STUCK LIKE THIS FOR THE *REST OF HER LIFE...?*
BECAUSE WE CAN'T LIFT THE SPELL MARA PUT ON MEGUMI UNLESS WE KNOW THE *PASSWORD...*
...AND THERE ARE AN ***INFINITE*** NUMBER OF POSSIBLE PASSWORD COMBINATIONS.
HEY!! HOW LONG ARE YOU GONNA KEEP ME WAITING ?!
HONK! HONK!
I'M A *CAR,* AND I EXPECT SOME ***DRIVE-THRU*** SERVICE!!
CALM DOWN, WILLYA?! I MEAN, HOW OFTEN DO YOU GET THE CHANCE TO TRY OUT A CAR LIKE *THAT?*
YOU INSENSITIVE ***JERK!!***
MAYBE YOU'D LIKE THIS TREAD ON YOUR ***PULL-OVER!***

AND SO...

...WE DECIDED WE'D BETTER FIGURE OUT A WAY TO CURE YOUR AMNESIA.
SORRY TO BE SO MUCH TROUBLE.

OKAY, *HERE'S* AN IDEA...
I'VE HEARD THE BEST CURE FOR MEMORY LOSS IS--

--A SUDDEN BLOW TO THE HEAD!!

YOU'VE BEEN WATCHING TOO MUCH DAY-TIME TV!
ARE YOU SURE *YOU'RE* NOT A DEMON, URD?
jeez
oop!
WHMP
THUD

WHAT ABOUT HOLDING YOUR BREATH AS LONG AS YOU CAN...
...OR DRINKING A GLASS OF WATER REALLY FAST?
I THINK THOSE ARE CURES FOR *HICCUPS*, BELL-DANDY.

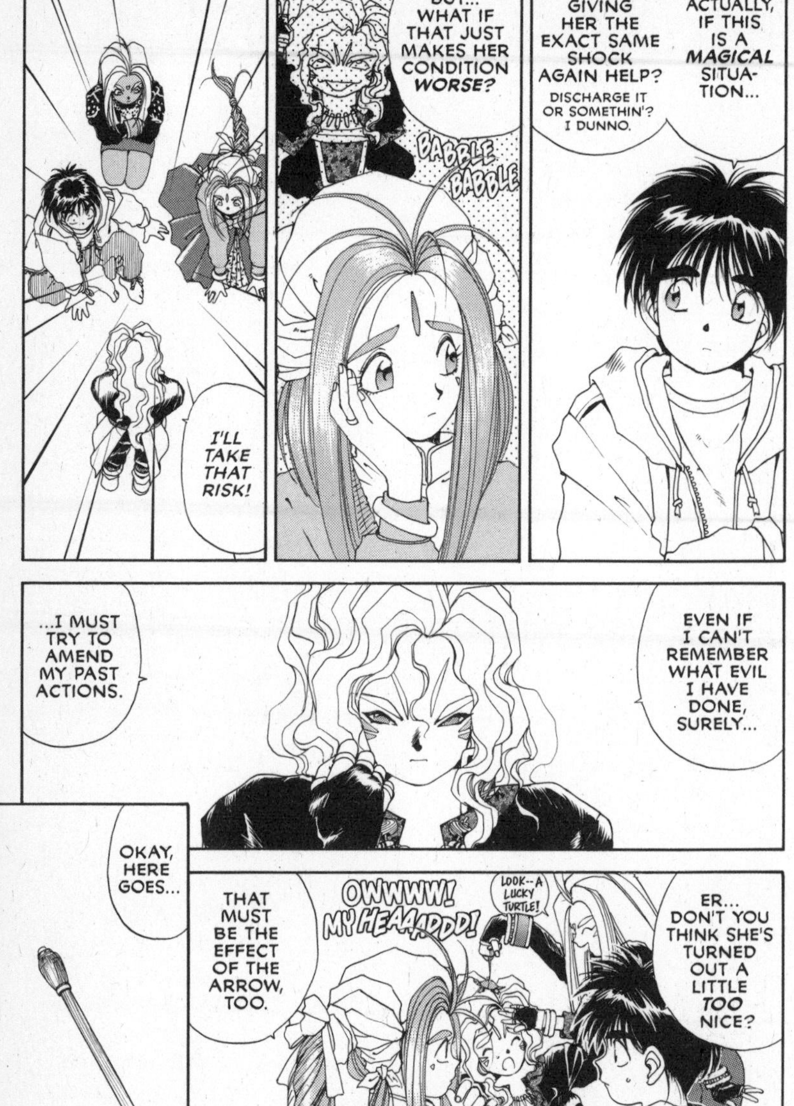
ACTUALLY, IF THIS IS A *MAGICAL* SITUATION...
...WOULD GIVING HER THE EXACT SAME SHOCK AGAIN HELP?
DISCHARGE IT OR SOMETHIN'? I DUNNO.
BUT... WHAT IF THAT JUST MAKES HER CONDITION *WORSE?*
BABBLE BABBLE
I'LL TAKE THAT RISK!
EVEN IF I CAN'T REMEMBER WHAT EVIL I HAVE DONE, SURELY...
...I MUST TRY TO AMEND MY PAST ACTIONS.
ER... DON'T YOU THINK SHE'S TURNED OUT A LITTLE *TOO* NICE?
LOOK--A LUCKY TURTLE!
OWWWW! MY HEAAADDD!
THAT MUST BE THE EFFECT OF THE ARROW, TOO.
OKAY, HERE GOES...

I'M SORRY...

OH, NO...

SHE'S STILL *POLITE?!* *IT DIDN'T WORK!*

...SHE MUST'VE ACQUIRED *IMMUNITY* TO THE ARROW-- IT CAN'T AFFECT HER ANYMORE!

OH, MARA! I'M NOT GOING TO ABANDON YOU.
YOU AND I HAVE KNOWN EACH OTHER SINCE CHILDHOOD.
IF IT WEREN'T FOR YOUR POOR SISTER, YOU COULD JUST LEAVE ME TO...TO F-FEND FOR... M-MYSELF...
ooohh
PLEASE FORGIVE ME...IF ONLY I COULD REMEMBER THE PASSWORD, EVERYTHING WOULD BE FINE!
BUT I...I JUST DON'T *KNOW!*
sniff sob
WAIT HERE, MARA.
I'LL THINK OF SOMETHING.
LUCKY *YOU,* MARA...

BLRRPLE
BLUP BLUP BLUP
HEE-HEE-HEE! YOU'LL RECOVER YOUR MEMORY IN A JIFFY...
...WITH URD'S SPECIAL AMNESIA ANTIDOTE, URDROGEN-X®!!

MARA, DEAREST!
SHIPP

EEEK!! STOP IT!!

WHAT?!

HONK! HONK!
WHADDAYA MEAN, "SHE RAN AWAY" ...?!
SLAM SLAM
ARGGH! YOU ALWAYS SCREW UP, KEIICHI!!
VROOM VROOM
WHSSSH
WELL, LET'S GO AFTER HER BEFORE SHE GETS TOO FAR.
!!
GACK! WHAT HAPPENED TO URD? HOW'D SHE GET SO SMALL?!
HEY, YOU'RE ONLY A TWO-SEATER... I LIKE COMFORT.
WAIT A SECOND! I GET IT!! YOU AND BELL-DANDY ARE...
...WITCH-ES!!
LIKE IN THAT TV SHOW!
WOW! GREAT! SO THIS MUST BE A DREAM !!

WHY, MEGUMI... I HADN'T THOUGHT OF THAT!

QUICK, LET'S HEAD OVER TO OTAKI'S PLACE!!

HE COLLECTS ALL *KINDS* OF JUNK LIKE THAT...

HOLD ON A SEC !!

HUH?

I'M THIRSTY !!

OH, OF COURSE! SHE'S OUT OF GAS!!

Z/100 SUPER PREMIUM

GASOLINE

FILL 'ER UP?

AND I WANT SUPER PREMIUM !!

OH, DEAR... I MUST'VE BEEN A REALLY *AWFUL* DEMON...
MAYBE... MAYBE IT'D BE BETTER IN THE LONG RUN IF I *NEVER* REGAIN MY MEMORY...
squeak
MARA !!
IF YOU DON'T GET YOUR MEMORY BACK, MEGUMI WILL BE LIKE THAT *FOREVER!!*
SHE'LL BE *VERY* EXPENSIVE TO MAINTAIN!!
FOR MEGUMI'S SAKE, YOU'VE *GOT* TO REMEMBER--

WHOOSSH
--AND FOR YOUR *OWN* SAKE, TOO!!
EEEYAAA
KRAK
shssshhhh
!
oooh...

DID YOU REALLY THINK THAT JUST BECAUSE YOU CURED ME, THAT I'D TELL YOU THE PASS-WORD?!
HAW HAW HAW!
FOOLS !!
...BUT WHAT WERE YOU THINK-ING?! HEH-HEH-HEH...!
THANK YOU...
...MY MIND IS NOW AS CLEAR AS AN UN-MUDDIED LAKE.

ONE PASSWORD LATER

CHAPTER 30

Engine O' Mystery

WINTER VACATION IS OVER, AND NEKOMI TECH'S STUDENTS ARE RETURNING TO CAMPUS... AND THE SHELTER OF THEIR DORMS.

OF COURSE, IN THIS BITTER SEASON, LET US REMEMBER...

猫実工大自動車部

...NOT ALL OF US HAVE SHELTER.

NOW LISSEN UP!!

THE (CURRENT SITE OF THE PREVIOUSLY BULLDOZED) *NEKOMI MOTOR CLUB*

猫実工大自動車部

FOR A MAN SUCH AS *ME*, DA HOWLIN' WIND IS NO DISCOMFORT! BUT WHUT ABOUT DA *WEAK?*
DA *PUNY?* YES, HOW LONG CAN *DEY* SURVIVE UNDER DESE CONDITIONS?!
ARE YOU ALL RIGHT, KEIICHI?
N-N-N-N-N-NEVER BETTER.
CHITTER CHATTER

WH-WH-WHAT ABOUT OUR P-P-PROCEEDS FROM THE CAMPUS FESTIVAL?
HM! OTAKI?

LESSEE... 1254 PEOPLE AT 200 YEN A HEAD--
--25,080 YEN GROSS.

MINUS 5150 YEN FOR *BEER AND SODA...*
...AND 15,400 YEN FOR THAT *BITCHIN' PAINT JOB* ON THE *SHINDEN...*
WE USED *SCHOOL* MATERIALS FOR THE RESTORATION WORK, SO *THAT* COST ZERO!!
...THAT'S 4530 NET.
grroaaann!
I FIGURED...
DON' *DESPAIR! YOU* CAN HELP!

NICE *PLAN,* TAMIYA!!

I CAN'T BELIEVE HE'S GOT US DOING *ENVELOPE STUFFING!*

BUT IT'S KIND OF FUN!

FOLD...

STUFF...

ONE HOUR LATER

FOLD...

STUFF...

ARRGGHH!! I'M GOING CRAZY! NUTS!! WE'LL NEVER RAISE THE MONEY LIKE THIS!!
IF ONLY THERE WAS ANOTHER WAY! IF ONLY!!
FZZAK
I HEARD THAT!
FRZZZLAKK
DO YOU WANT TO MAKE MORE MONEY? SURE! WE ALL DO!
...WHAT'S THAT LOOK FOR?
GEE...
...WHAT LOOK?
ANYWAY, LEAVE EVERYTHING TO ME! I'M FEELIN' LUCKY TONIGHT!!

Come, O Six Gods of Fortune...
KASHING!
...And Form... Super Combo-Lucky-God!!
RMBB
RMBB
KASHING!
1. LUCKY MALLET
2. LUCKY BADGER
3. LUCKY DOLPHIN
4. LUCKY CAT'S PAW
5. LUCKY GNOME'S CAPE
6. LUCKY BANNER
WHAM!

HOW'S THAT?!
...!

WITH THIS THING GIVING YOU GOOD FORTUNE...
...YOU'LL BE MAKING THAT MONEY IN NO TIME!

I DUNNO... NORMAL PEOPLE ARE GONNA THINK THIS THING IS PRETTY WEIRD...
KEIICHI !!
LISSEN, YOU GOTTA LEMME HAVE IT! I'LL PAY YOU ANY-THING!
WOTTA FIND FOR MY COLLEC-TION!!
ON SECOND THOUGHT, MAYBE WE'LL KEEP IT.

ONE OF YOU SIGN FOR THIS?
NEKOMI SOME-THIN' CLUB...?

BRUB

HMM...

WHAT IS IT?
HUH?

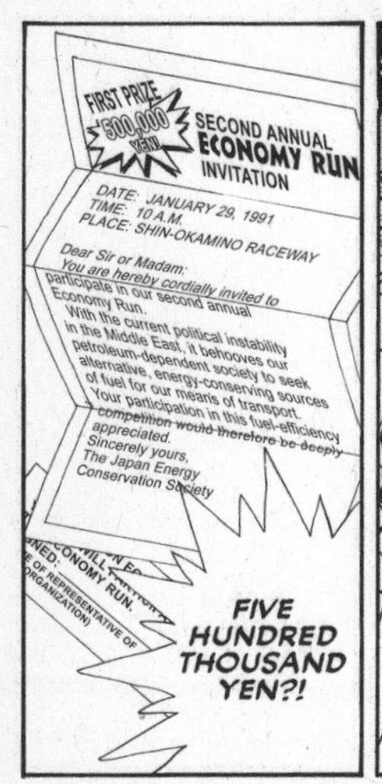
FIRST PRIZE
500,000 YEN
SECOND ANNUAL
ECONOMY RUN
INVITATION
DATE: JANUARY 29, 1991
TIME: 10 A.M.
PLACE: SHIN-OKAMINO RACEWAY
Dear Sir or Madam:
You are hereby cordially invited to participate in our second annual Economy Run.
With the current political instability in the Middle East, it behooves our petroleum-dependent society to seek alternative, energy-conserving sources of fuel for our means of transport.
Your participation in this fuel-efficiency competition would therefore be deeply appreciated.
Sincerely yours,
The Japan Energy Conservation Society
FIVE HUNDRED THOUSAND YEN?!

WOW !!

THE "JAPAN ENERGY CONSERVATION SOCIETY" ...?
huh?

FORTUNE HAS OPENED ITS *BIG GAPIN' MOUTH* T' *SMILE* UPON US!
DAT'S HOW WE'S GONNA REBUILD OUR CLUB-HOUSE!

HOW COME YOU DIDN'T MENTION THIS CONTEST BEFORE?

I DIN'T KNOW ABOUT IT! YOU ENTER US, OTAKI?

NOPE! LET'S SEE THAT ENVE-LOPE...

!!

NEKOMI TECH FOUR WHEELS CLUB
18-7 UMATEBUKURO, UEKIJO-CHO,
NEKOMI CITY, JAPAN

WHAT DO WE *DO*?

THERE'S ONLY ONE *THING* TO DO...

...DESTROY DA EVIDENCE!!

WE NEVER SAW NO ENVELOPE!

RIP RIP RIP

DAT CASH NOW BELONGS TO DA *NEKOMI TECH MOTOR CLUB!!*

HUZZAH!!

HMPH!! THOSE ROTTEN MOTOR CLUB THIEVES!! DON'T THEY HAVE ANY *SHAME?*

WE'D BETTER TELL PRESIDENT AOSHIMA ABOUT *THIS!!*

NIT FWC

猫実工大四輪部

...THANK YOU, MY LOVELY SPIES.

HMM... I SEE.

I *WAS* PLANNING TO GRIND THEM **FURTHER** INTO THE MUD BY **WINNING** THAT MONEY FOR OUR CLUB, BUT...

WELL... THERE'S MORE THAN ONE WAY TO SKIN A GEEK.

LET THEM BE.

YES... ***ALLOW*** THEM TO ENTER THE RACE...

SIR?

KZZZZZ
WHAT-CHA DOIN'?
TRYING TO MAKE THE CONNECT-ING ROD LIGHTER...

ACROSS CAMPUS...
N.I.T F.W.C
NEKOMI INSTITUTE OF TECHNOLOGY
FOUR WHEELS CLUB

YO, MORISATO-- I'M GONNA GO PICK US UP SOME ALUMINUM FRAME MATERIAL.
"PICK IT UP"? FROM WHERE?

I WANNA MILL THE HEAD AND PISTON CROWN TOO, BUT I CAN'T 'CAUSE THAT WOULD UP THE DIS-PLACEMENT. A PORT 'N' POLISH IS OKAY, THOUGH.
WHAT I'D LIKE TO DO IS GET A CERAMIC ROD AND PISTON, BUT THERE'S NO TIME, SO...
...THEN I'M GONNA PUT IN SPLIT-ELECTRODE TWIN PLUGS TO UP THE FUEL EFFI-CIENCY.

DON'T WORRY ABOUT ALL THOSE LITTLE DETAILS!
JUST LEAVE IT UP TO THE TROLLS WHO POWER THE ENGINE, OKAY?
...
TROLLS?
REALLY... THESE GODDESSES...

NOW WE GOTTA HIT... I MEAN, HIT UP, DA THE BICYCLE CLUB FOR SOME *WHEELS!!*
AWRIGHT, WE GOT DA SOOPAH-STRUC-TURE!
HUZZAH #2!
WHATEVER IT TAKES!!
NOW *I'M* FREEZING!
crumple
THIEVES!
....
fwap
WE BORROWE
YOUR WINDO
FRAMES.
SIGNED,
THE MOTOR C
ANONYMOU

CHALLENGE TO MINIMUM

ECONOMY RUN

GRAND PRIZE

500 THOUSAND YEN

THE ECONOMY RUN...

...IS BASICALLY A FUEL CONSERVATION CONTEST.

CAR INSPECTI

EACH CAR CARRIES ONE LITER OF GAS AND GOES A FIXED DISTANCE WITHIN A FIXED PERIOD OF TIME.

NEKOMI TECH MOTOR CLUB? LESSEE...

...OKAY. YOU PASSED.

T'ANKS...

THE CAR THAT USES UP THE LEAST FUEL WINS.

OH!
HOW DID THE INSPECTION GO?
WE ACED IT!!
EVEN BY THIS CLUB'S STANDARDS...
...I GOTTA ADMIT, THIS IS ONE WEIRD MACHINE.
YES...
...IT IS A BIT ODD, ISN'T IT?

AOSHIMA!!
ON THE OTHER HAND...
...OUR CLUB'S MACHINE LOOKS QUITE RESPECTABLE.
AND WE DID IT *WITHOUT* WINDOW FRAMES.
WHAT DO YOU SAY TO A WAGER?
NIT FWC
00

IT AIN'T NO *WAGER*... IT'S A ***BET!***
...BUT IF *WE* ***LOSE***, WE DON'T LOSE ***NUTHIN'***... CUZ *WE GOT* NUTHIN'!!
AIEE!! ***NO!!***
MMM... LESSEE... DAT MEANS... DUH...IF ***WE*** *WIN, WE GET DA PRIZE MONEY* ***AN'*** *A WHOLE NEW CLUBHOUSE...*
NO, TAMIYA! ***DON'T*** USE YOUR BRAIN!
THE *WINNING* TEAM...
...GETS TO TAKE OVER THE ***LOSING*** TEAM'S CLUB-HOUSE!

ECONOMY RUN RUN '91
START
5 MINUTES TO STARTING TIME!
5 MINUTES TO STARTING TIME!
ALL CARS, LINE UP ON THE GRID!!

BE CAREFUL, BELL-DANDY...

...WE'VE GOT TO ASSUME THAT AOSHIMA HAS SOMETHING UP HIS DESIGNER SLEEVE.

AND BESIDES...

DON'T WORRY, KEIICHI.

WE HAVE *THIS* ADVANTAGE... I'M THE LIGHTEST DRIVER IN THE RACE.

HOW COULD THEY POSSIBLY HOPE TO BEAT OUR EXPENSIVE TITANIUM AND CARBON-FIBER RACER?!
DID YOU DO AS INSTRUCT-ED?
YES, SIR!

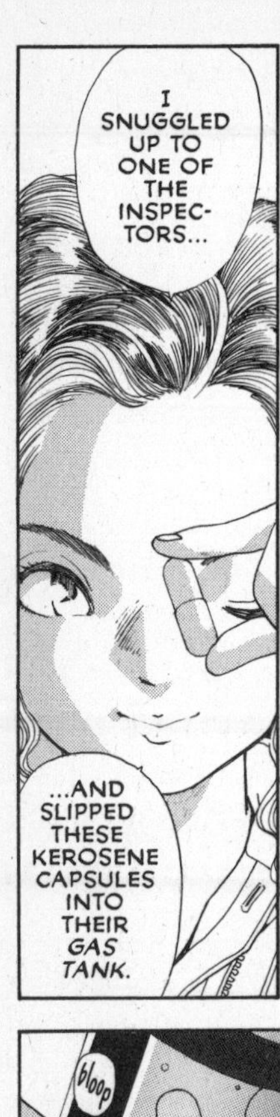
I SNUGGLED UP TO ONE OF THE INSPEC-TORS...
...AND SLIPPED THESE KEROSENE CAPSULES INTO THEIR GAS TANK.

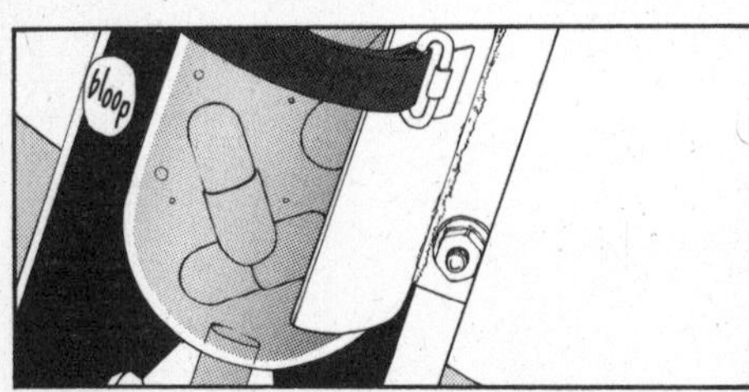
bloop

C-5!!
DAMN! A DIRECT HIT!!

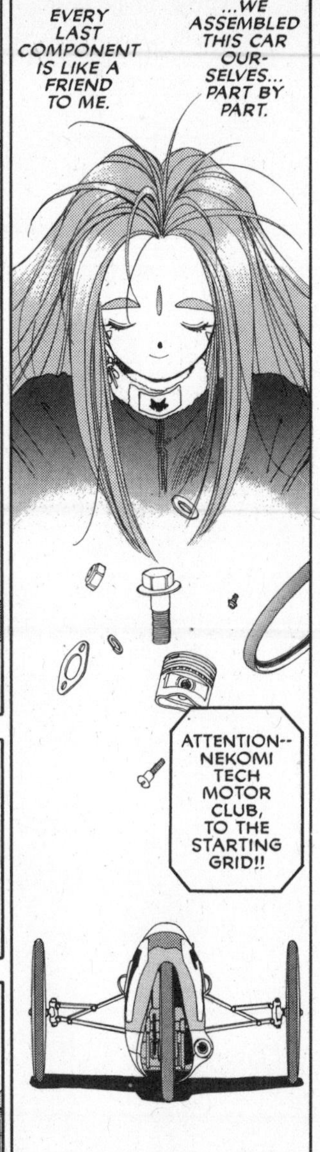
...WE ASSEMBLED THIS CAR OUR-SELVES... PART BY PART.
EVERY LAST COMPONENT IS LIKE A FRIEND TO ME.
ATTENTION--NEKOMI TECH MOTOR CLUB, TO THE STARTING GRID!!

C'MON, GUYS, GET SERIOUS!!
HUH? WHY?
IT'S ALL UP TO BELL NOW, ANYWAY!
HIGH SPIRITS
YUASA

FWHOOOSSHH
IN AN ECONOMY RACE, YOU DON'T WANT TO RUN YOUR ENGINE ALL THE TIME.
7
NIT MCC

INSTEAD, YOU ACCELERATE, THEN COAST...
...REPEATING THE PROCESS IN A CYCLE.
7

OKAY, FELLOWS... YOUR NAP IS OVER...

...LET'S GO AGAIN !!
FSSSHHH

CHIBA COLLEGE WE NEVER LOSE
!!

SPUT SPUT SPUT

OH, NO!
W-WHAT'S WRONG ?!

KEIICHI!! THE ENGINE ...!
BELL ?!

TAMIYA! OTAKI! HELP!

SNORE! ZZZ---Z!
AH, NEVER MIND.

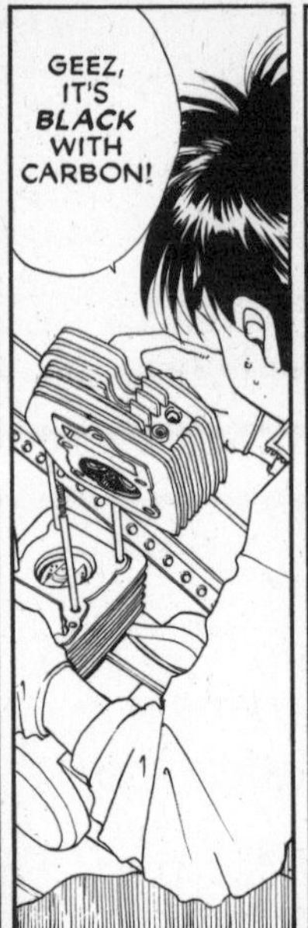
GEEZ, IT'S *BLACK* WITH CARBON!

ARE THOSE TROLLS GOOFING OFF?
NOT *THAT* AGAIN.

HMM, PERHAPS THAT'S IT, URD...
UH... BELLDANDY.

KLAK

WHOOSH
UM...

UH-
OH!

WHY
AREN'T
YOU BOYS
WORKING
LIKE YOU
SHOULD?
GIBBER! TROLLS! HA-HA! TROLLS IN THE ENGINE!
heh-
heh!

RMBL
'CAUSE
WE'RE
NAUGHTY
OLD
TROLLS!
URD
!!
LET'S
GET
'EM!

DIVIDE AND CAPTURE !!
SPROING

GRAB!
GACK !!
Belldandy Super Attraction!
ALL ACCOUNTED FOR?
OH, DEAR. ONE'S STILL MISSING.
NO, THAT TECHNIQUE ONLY WORKS IF THEY'RE STILL CLOSE BY...
hahh
hah
LOOKS LIKE I GOT AWAY...
OOH...
OOH, THE PAIN...
THE PAIN... *IN MY HEART...*
!!

OOH...
PLEASE...
...I BEG YOU...
...TOUCH ME...
sigh

T-T-*TOUCH* YOU ...?!
WHERE? ***WHERE?***

STOMP STOMP STOMP
ON THE BOTTOM OF MY *HEELS*, SUCKER.

NOW, TELL ME-- *WHY* DID YOU BOYS SLACK OFF ON THE JOB?
'CAUSE A' *DIS* CRAP !!

...THAT WAS AN ACT OF SABOTAGE BY...BY THE *BIG MONEY MEN!!*
PLEASE BELIEVE ME...
AOSHIMA!! THAT *SCUM!*
EVEN IF HE *DIDN'T* DO IT... HE'S *STILL* SCUM!
huh? SMELLS LIKE *KEROSENE!!*
HOW'S YA EXPECT US T' DO OUR JOBS WIT' DESE *IMPURITIES?* IT'S AGAINST TROLL UNION *REGULATIONS!*
OH, *HO!* EXPLOITERS A' DA WOIKIN' TROLL, AY? DEY TINK DEY CAN JOIK US AROUN' LIKE DAT?
C'MON, BOYS! WE GONNA SHOW *DEM* WHO MOVES DA WORLD!!!

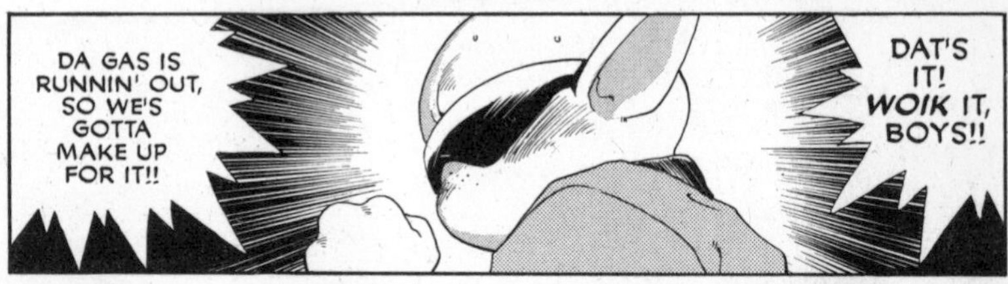

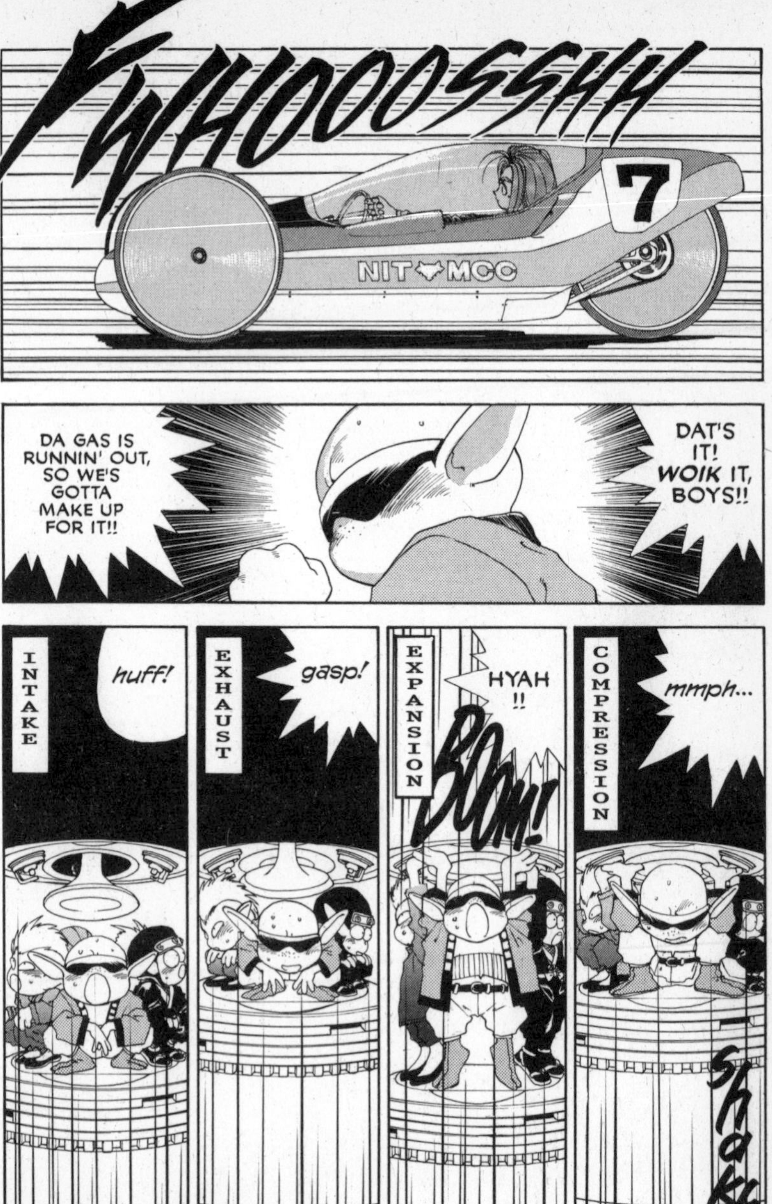

COMPRESSION

mmph...

SHAKE

EXPANSION

HYAH!!

BOOM!

EXHAUST

gasp!

INTAKE

huff!

(REPEAT 1500 TIMES PER MINUTE = 3000RPM)

HUP-TWO-THREE-FOUR!!
HUP-TWO-THREE-FOUR!!
HUP-TWO-THREE-FOUR!!
HUP-TWO-THREE-FOUR!!
POOR (and I do mean *poor*) ***FOOLS!!*** AT THAT PACE THEY'LL USE UP FAR TOO MUCH FUEL!!
BUT...
UMATEGAWA UNIVERSITY
NEKOMI TECH FOUR WHEELS CLUB
NEKOMI TECH MOTOR CLUB
WE... ***WE DID IT!!***
URK!
AND THE WINNER IS--***THE NEKOMI TECH MOTOR CLUB!!***
huh? OVER AW-READY?
....
BUT... BUT HOW?
1
BUT THE CLUB-HOUSE WON BY THE MOTOR CLUB...
...HAD NO WINDOW FRAMES.
HEY!! IS YOU TRYIN' TA ***RIP US OFF?!***
RANT
RAGE!
B-B-BUT... *YOU* TOOK THEM!

NEXT TIME IN OH MY GODDESS!

Oh My Goddess!
ああっ女神さまっ
藤島康介
5

VOLUME 5 ISBN: 1-84576-506-0 ISBN-13: 978-1-84576-506-4

ALSO AVAILABLE

VOLUME 1
ISBN: 1-84576-485-4
ISBN-13: 978-1-84576-485-2

VOLUME 2
ISBN: 1-84576-486-2
ISBN-13: 978-1-84576-486-9

VOLUME 3
ISBN: 1-84576-504-4
ISBN-13: 978-1-84576-504-0